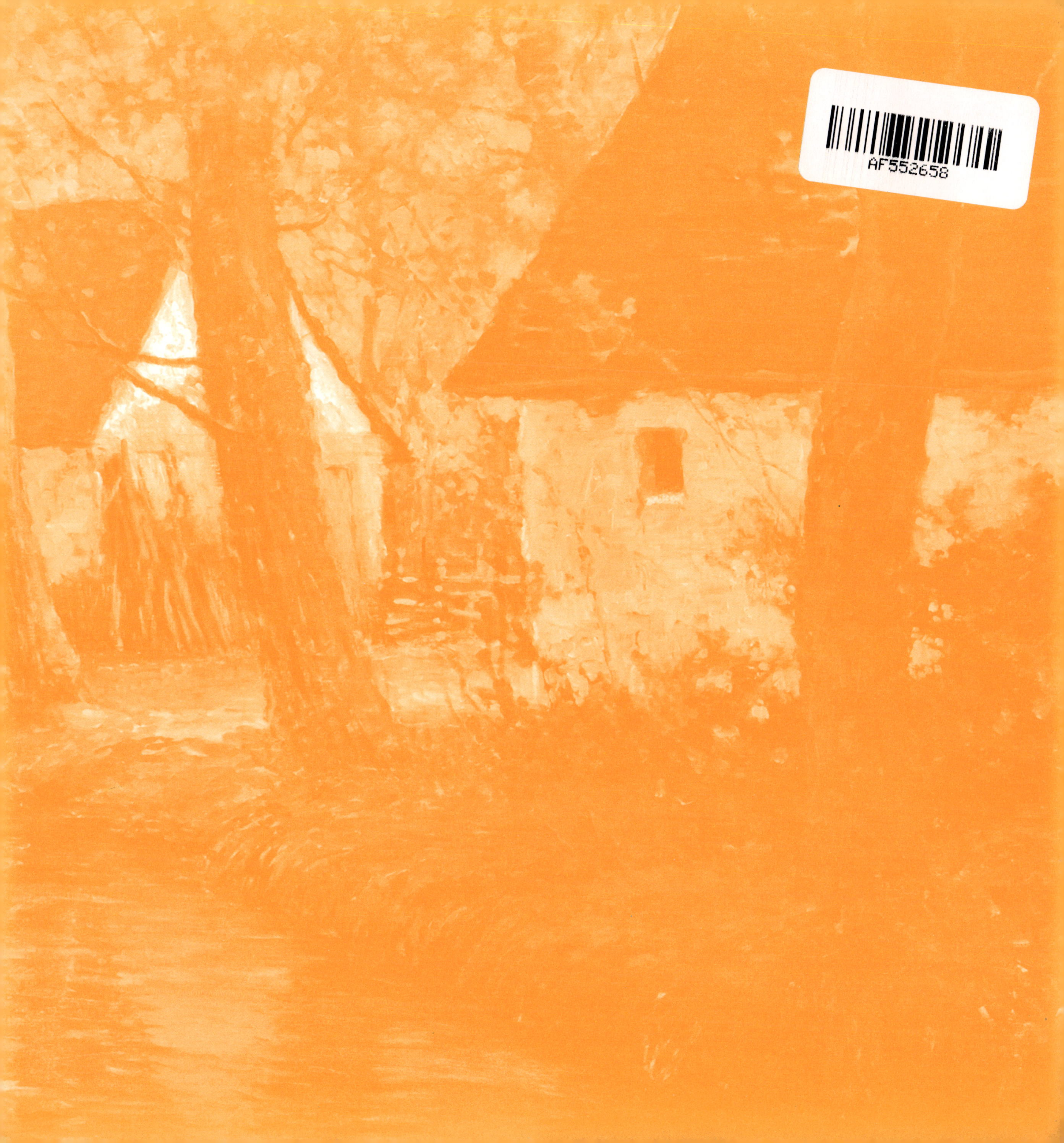
AF552658

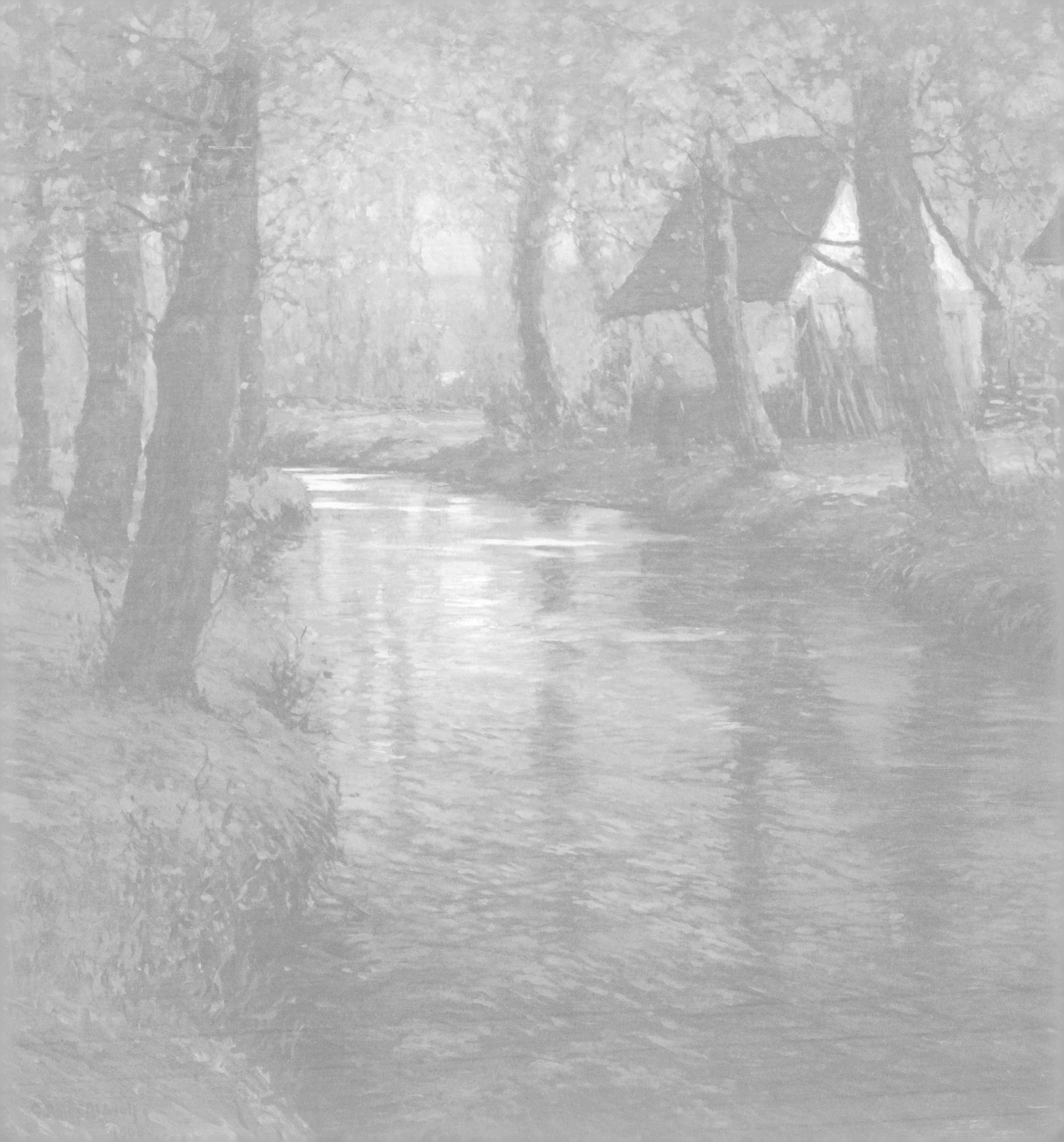

THE ART OF GEORGE AMES ALDRICH

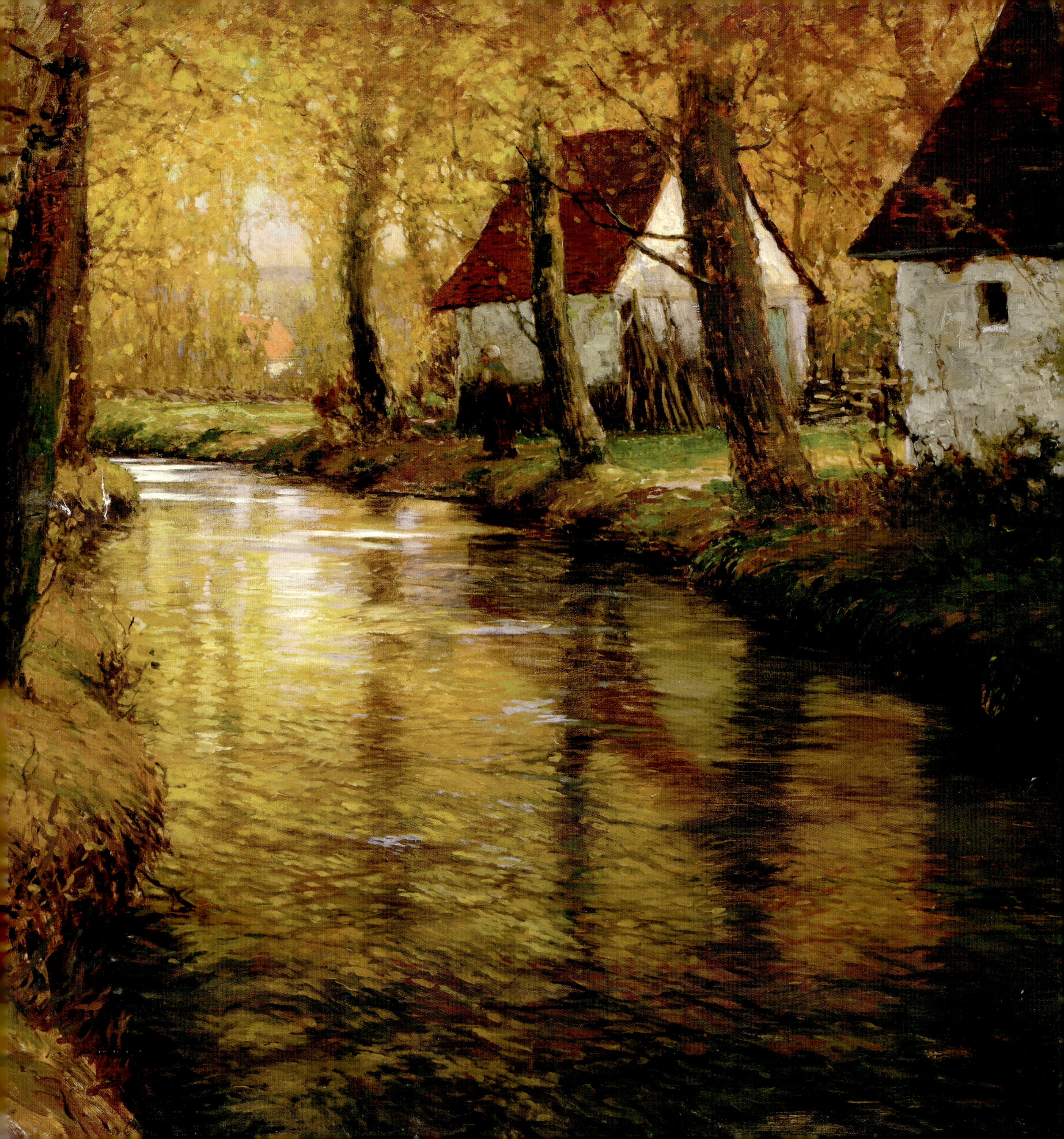

The Art of George Ames Aldrich

WENDY GREENHOUSE

WITH CONTRIBUTIONS BY

GREGG HERTZLIEB

AND

MICHAEL WRIGHT

INDIANA UNIVERSITY PRESS *Bloomington & Indianapolis*

This book is a publication of

INDIANA UNIVERSITY PRESS
601 North Morton Street
Bloomington, Indiana 47404-3797 USA

iupress.indiana.edu

Telephone orders 800-842-6796
Fax orders 812-855-7931

∞ The paper used in this publication meets the minimum requirements of the American National Standard for Information Sciences – Permanence of Paper for Printed Library Materials, ANSI Z39.48–1992.

Manufactured in China

Library of Congress
Cataloging-in-Publication Data

Greenhouse, Wendy, [date]
The art of George Ames Aldrich / Wendy Greenhouse ; with contributions by Gregg Hertzlieb and Michael Wright.
pages cm
Issued in connection with an exhibition of the artist's paintings, held 2012 at the Brauer Museum of Art, Valparaiso University, Valparaiso, Indiana.
Includes bibliographical references.
ISBN 978-0-253-00905-0 (cloth : alk. paper) – ISBN 978-0-253-00913-5 (ebook) 1. Aldrich, George Ames, 1871-1941 – Exhibitions. I. Brauer Museum of Art. II. Title.
ND237.A34A4 2013
759.13 – dc23

2012051723

1 2 3 4 5 18 17 16 15 14 13

GEORGE AMES ALDRICH

CONTENTS

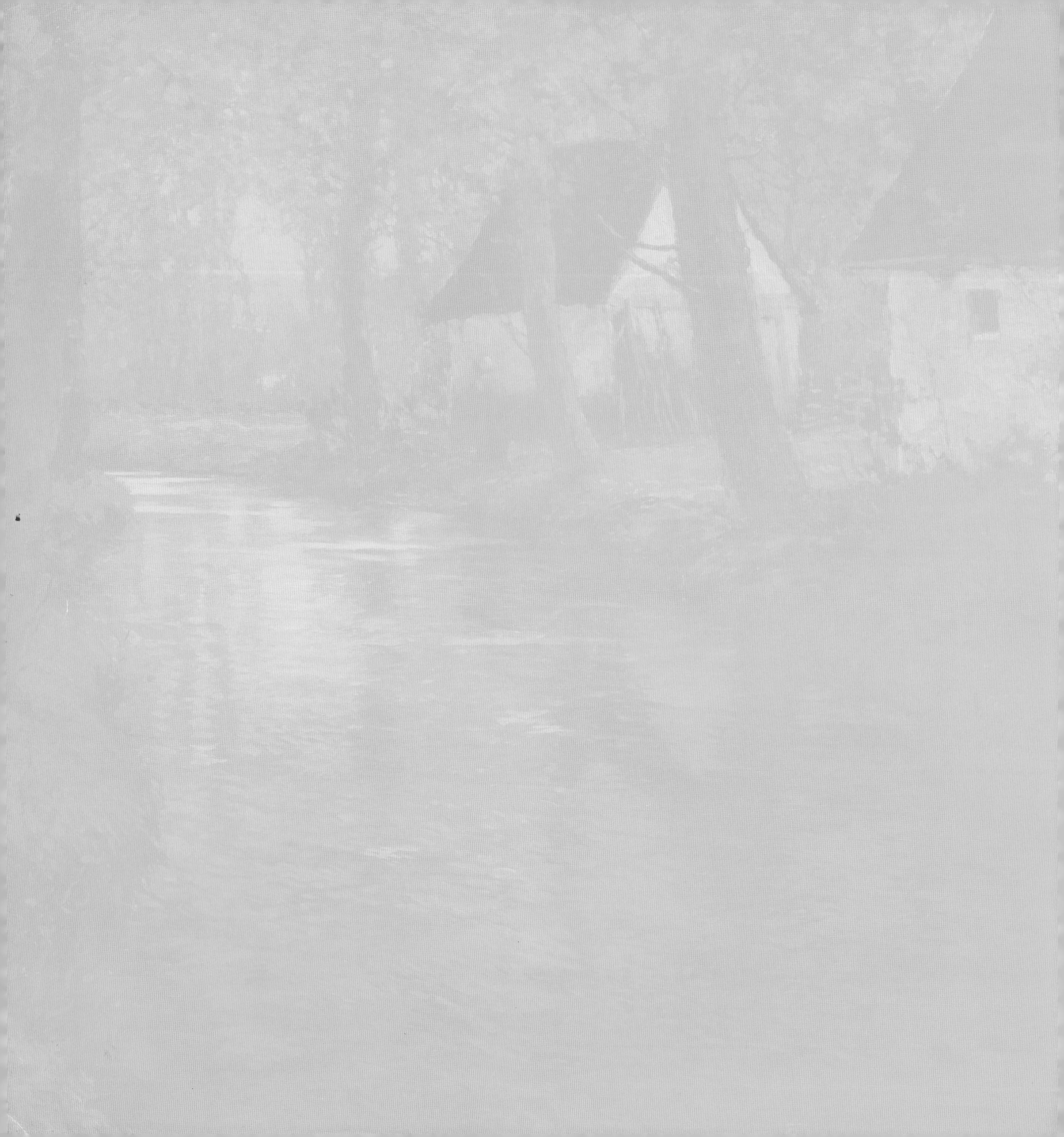

THE ART OF GEORGE AMES ALDRICH

INTRODUCTION & ACKNOWLEDGMENTS

THE LIFE AND WORK OF ARTIST GEORGE AMES Aldrich (1871–1941) are the focus of this book, produced in conjunction with a major 2012 exhibition of the artist's paintings at the Brauer Museum of Art, Valparaiso University. A highly regarded artist, Aldrich drew upon his years of experience living and studying in Europe to create beautiful landscape paintings, particularly scenes of northern France. He began his career in Europe as an illustrator and through study and practice became increasingly skilled in his romantic representations of the land and water in the peaceful French countryside. Aldrich moved to the Chicago area in 1915 and then lived for several years in South Bend, Indiana, before returning to Chicago. He won several awards for his art, which he exhibited at the Art Institute of Chicago, the Hoosier Salon, the Chicago Galleries Association, and elsewhere. In South Bend, Aldrich remains a legendary figure who contributed much to the history of art in Indiana.

Michael Wright, curator of the 2012 exhibition, assembled many of Aldrich's strongest works for the artist's first-ever retrospective, identifying key pieces in public and private collections, some representing French subjects but others depicting the Midwestern steel industry and American nature. The essays in this volume by Wendy Greenhouse, assisted by Michael, explore in detail Aldrich's life, influences, sources of inspiration, and art-historical context, shedding new light on the career of an artist whose works continue to impress and delight collectors and viewers.

We are grateful to numerous individuals and organizations who made the exhibition and this publication possible. First and foremost is Peter Lundberg of Janus Galleries, Madison, Wisconsin, who has done considerable research on Aldrich and generously shared it for this project, which would not have been possible without his expertise. Peter provided invaluable access to Aldrich's scrapbook as well as his files and manuscript biography of the artist. Our thanks also go to Richard Brauer, William Briska, Jan Cover of Purdue University, Gary Cialdella, Joel Dryer, Richard and Phyllis Duesenberg, Mike Ficheel of the Aurora Historical Society, Patti Gilford, Bronislaus Janulis, Michael Koryta, Michael A. Nickol, Richard Norton and Susan Klein-Bagdad of Richard Norton

Gallery in Chicago, Dean Porter, Oslo art consultant Vidar Poulsson, Monica and Ronald Radecki, and Jim Ross. We also acknowledge the assistance of the staff of Indiana University Press, the Ryerson and Burnham Libraries at the Art Institute of Chicago, and the Local History and Genealogy Collection at the South Bend Public Library. At the Brauer Museum, the project was ably managed and assisted by Gloria Ruff, Danielle Ren Hertzlieb, and Aran Kessler. At Valparaiso University, we are grateful for the institutional support of President Mark Heckler, Provost Mark Schwehn, and Associate Provost Renu Juneja. The staff of Valparaiso University's Office of Integrated Marketing and Communications provided essential promotional services, and the Partners for the Brauer Museum of Art generously underwrote the project.

We are also grateful to the lenders to the exhibition: Richard and Jean Dennen; the Charles S. Hayes family; Brian Kastman and Ann Rohrbaugh; Bernie and Sue Konrady; Martin and Debbie Radecki; Drs. Nicole and Todd Rozycki; the Saunders family; Mary Toll and Bill Heimann; Bradley Vite; Matthew M. Walsh; Mark Forrest West; the Art Museum of Greater Lafayette; the Snite Museum of Art, University of Notre Dame; the South Bend Museum of Art; First Financial Bank, N.A.; Clifford Law Offices, Chicago; Elgin Mental Health Center; the Sioux City Art Center; and an anonymous lender.

We deeply appreciate the enthusiasm and support of all involved in the George Ames Aldrich project. Through their efforts, we all are able to gain a better understanding of Aldrich's life and creations.

GREGG HERTZLIEB, Director/Curator
Brauer Museum of Art, Valparaiso University

A BIOGRAPHY

WENDY GREENHOUSE

WITH MICHAEL WRIGHT

FOR AN ARTIST WHO MADE INNUMERABLE SALES OF his artworks, won prizes, belonged to artists' organizations, circulated socially among his potential patrons, and assiduously cultivated press attention, George Ames Aldrich remains a somewhat elusive figure. Much of what we think we know about the artist, especially regarding his training, early career, and travels, is uncertain or disputed. Ironically, Aldrich's life is relatively well documented. Although almost none of his correspondence or sketches survive, a scrapbook of newspaper clippings and other ephemera compiled by his wife Esta facilitates reconstruction of many of his professional activities at least for the years he was most active in the Midwest, between 1919 and the mid-1930s. Aldrich listed himself in several editions of the *American Art Directory,* occasionally wrote for publication, and actively sought venues for the exhibition and sale of his paintings. Twice married, he was by all accounts no recluse but a charming, gregarious individual. Yet research reveals numerous contradictions and apparent outright fictions in the record of his career. His typically romantic paintings, rarely dated or datable from their subject matter, provide few further clues. The account presented here greatly expands on and corrects previous ones, but it also suggests that much remains to be learned about Aldrich's life. What does emerge is a picture of an artist drawn to self-invention and to creative fictionalizing of a piece with his characteristic romantic images.

The very year of Aldrich's birth is uncertain: he supplied either 1871 or 1872 on different occasions, although 1871 is evidently correct.[1] He was born George Eugene Aldrich in Worcester, Massachusetts, the elder son of George Wellington Aldrich, a dry goods merchant, and Caroline Richmond Ames Aldrich, a dressmaker.[2] Aldrich attended Dean Academy, a college preparatory school in Franklin, Massachusetts, where he graduated in 1889.[3] He was widely reported to have studied architecture at the Massachusetts Institute of Technology, although that institution has no record of him. In the autumn of 1891, Aldrich enrolled in New York's Art Students League, where his teachers may have included William Merritt Chase, Henry Siddons Mowbray, and John Twachtman.[4] His contact with any of them was necessarily brief, however,

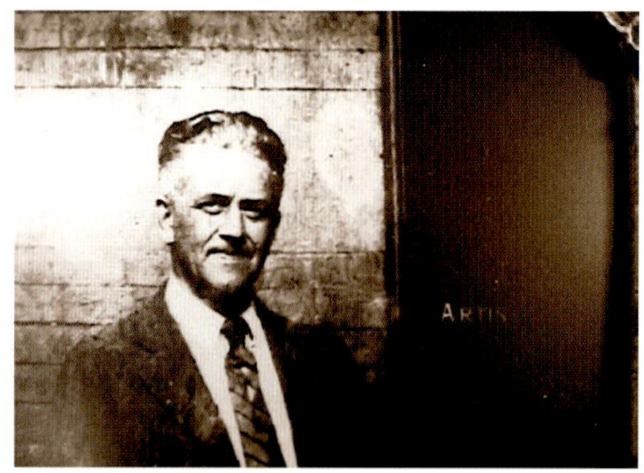

Aldrich photographed outside the Makielski Art Shop when it was located in the Oliver Theatre Building, South Bend, ca. 1920.

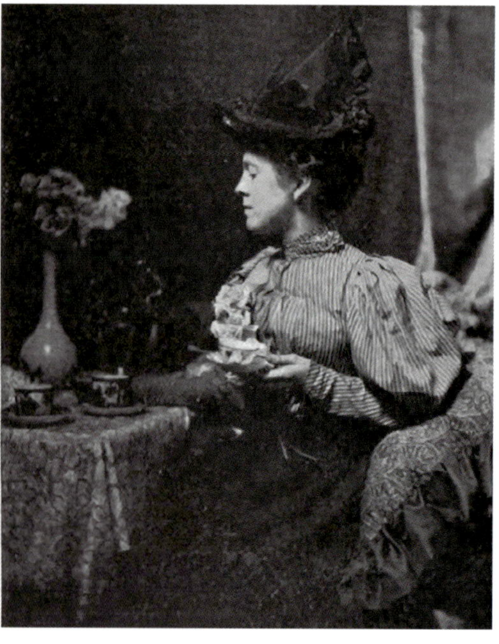

1.1. Aldrich's photograph *Afternoon Tea,* reproduced in *The Quarterly Illustrator* 2 (July–September 1894), 324.

as he remained in the school barely six months. The following summer, a Worcester newspaper noted that Aldrich had received praise for skill in pen-and-ink drawing, which would soon lead him into a career as an illustrator.[5] He was said to be planning to exhibit oil paintings in an upcoming exhibition at the Boston Art Club, but there is no record that he did so.[6]

In 1894, a magazine on illustration reproduced a photographic figure study by Aldrich (Figure 1.1), suggesting that he was experimenting with a new medium.[7] Yet his fine art ambitions evidently remained: later that year he departed for Europe for an anticipated three-year stay that stretched to 1900.[8] In Paris, he followed the usual course for American art students, enrolling in the Académie Julian and the Académie Colarossi; he also attended "private classes of some well-known artists."[9] His teachers included academic painter Raphaël Collin, Symbolist artist Edmond Aman-Jean, and as many as four others, suggesting that he flitted somewhat from one studio and academy to another.[10] All were primarily figural artists, but very few examples of Aldrich's figure painting survive.[11] He also claimed to have studied with James McNeill Whistler, although this too cannot be substantiated. Nominally the proprietor of the short-lived Académie Carmen in Paris, the famous American expatriate artist had little direct interaction with the students there; nor is Aldrich known to have been among the numerous etchers who came into contact with him in his role as a master printmaker.[12] To have been Whistler's student was a coveted credential that Aldrich may have invented on the basis of an actual if fleeting connection – or none at all.[13] Regardless, his interest both in etching and in the shadowy tones and nocturnal settings of Tonalism, a widely influential mode in the years he began to paint landscapes, reflects the general influence of Whistler, who remained a towering figure in the international art world at the turn of the twentieth century.

Aldrich's charcoal self-portrait (Plate 1) may date to his years in France. Showing the artist as a rather romantic figure, with shaggy hair, drooping mustache, and upturned gaze, it demonstrates his facility as a draftsman and command of portraiture. Aldrich put these skills to work in the late 1890s as an illustrator for several English and American periodicals

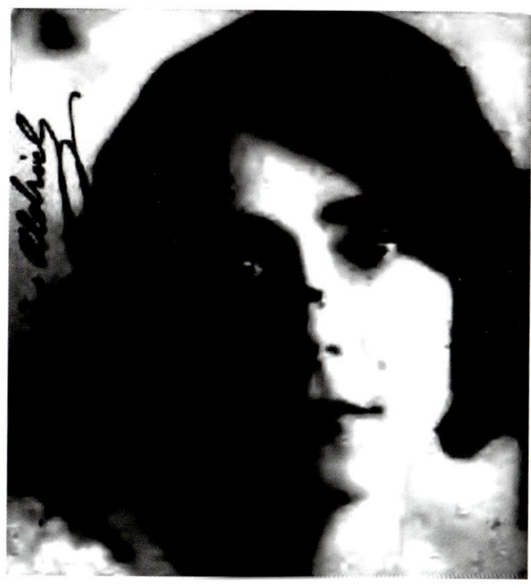

1.2. Eugenie Wehrle Aldrich, from a photograph in a passport application, 1920.

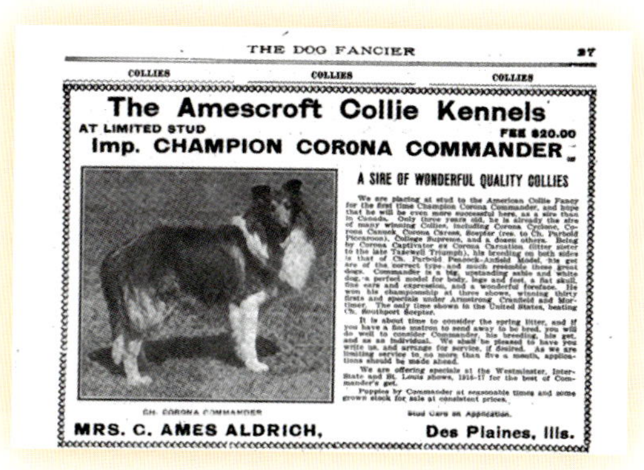

1.3. Advertisement for Amescroft Kennels, Des Plaines, Illinois, in *Dog Fancier* 24 (December 1915), 27. Library of the University of Wisconsin, Madison.

that may have included the London *Times, Punch,* and the American magazines *Life, Truth,* and *Vogue.*[14] Around 1904, however, his focus returned to painting as he began to make landscapes, reportedly under the influence of painter Fritz Thaulow, according to numerous accounts that all originated with Aldrich. These go so far as to claim that the two "painted as companions in France" during the last two years of Thaulow's life, which ended in 1906.[15] During that period, however, the Norwegian artist was almost entirely absent from France, one of several facts that cast considerable doubt on Aldrich's story.[16] On the other hand, he certainly studied Thaulow's celebrated paintings, which were widely exhibited as well as reproduced from the mid-1890s onward.

Between 1904 and 1910, Aldrich made several short stays in France.[17] Independent of later accounts that he supplied, his activities there are undocumented. Titles of his paintings indicate that he may have worked in several settings in Brittany, Normandy, Artois, and Picardy, as well as Holland. Few of his early landscapes are dated, however, and therefore they shed little light on his travels. The seaside Normandy town of Dieppe served as his base, but he later claimed as his "home" Montreuil-sur-Mer, some sixty miles away; both had long been the haunts of artists.[18] After-the-fact accounts that Aldrich exhibited in Paris and that he was a member of the Société des Artistes Français – one of his proudest claims – are not borne out by available records.[19]

By September 1906 Aldrich had changed his middle name, Eugene, to the more distinctive Ames (his mother's maiden name), perhaps to highlight his roots in one of Massachusetts' founding families.[20] He had returned from France a few months earlier accompanied by a Mrs. Aldrich, according to the ship manifest – no doubt the former Eugenie Wehrle, a fellow artist (Figure 1.2).[21] In New York Aldrich's paintings were displayed on the premises of an aspiring art dealer and offered for sale by a department store, but he did not appear in the city's mainstream exhibition venues and made no visible mark on its professional art life.[22]

Aldrich made at least two more return visits to Europe, in 1908 and 1910.[23] In the United States, meanwhile, he and his wife led a somewhat peripatetic life as the painter mingled art with other endeavors. New York, Philadelphia, Worcester, and Duxbury, Massachusetts, may have been their homes at various times.[24] Aldrich designed theater curtains and sets in Altoona, Pennsylvania, an activity possibly connected with Eugenie's aspirations for a stage career, and he pursued commercial reproduction of his paintings.[25] Yet when the couple traveled to Winnipeg and California on "professional business" in 1915, its nature was not artistic but canine, for by then they had already spent five years "in the Collie game."[26] Advertisements for Amescroft Kennels, Mrs. G. Ames Aldrich proprietor (Figure 1.3), and frequent "Collie Notes by Amescroft" penned by the artist for the magazine *Dog Fancier* document George and Eugenie's brief but serious shared career as collie breeders.[27] In late 1915, Amescroft Kennels set up shop in Des Plaines, Illinois, where the couple had a longstanding acquaintance, but less than two years later they settled in the middle-class Woodlawn neighborhood on Chicago's South Side.[28] Although he moved repeatedly, Aldrich would retain his ties to the Woodlawn–Hyde Park area for the rest of his life.

During his years as a dog breeder Aldrich maintained a parallel identity as a professional artist. He even mingled the two when he offered his landscape paintings as prizes in three consecutive annual competitions of the St. Louis Collie Club.[29] He first appeared on Chicago's art scene in 1915, when one of his typical stream-and-cottage paintings was among several hundred artworks purchased by the owner of the Congress Hotel to decorate guestrooms.[30] Works by Aldrich found their way into J. W. Young's State Street gallery and a 1917 exhibition at the Tri-City Art League in Davenport, Iowa, organized by the Art Institute of Chicago's Extension Department.[31] Amescroft Kennels was officially dissolved in late 1917, and early the following year Aldrich made his debut in the Art Institute's important *Chicago and Vicinity* exhibition, where he would be represented almost annually for a decade (in 1921 he showed for the only time in the American art annual).[32] At the same time Eugenie, who had begun painting in France, enrolled in the Art Institute's school.

The year 1919 marked Aldrich's full emergence as a professional artist in Chicago. He began sharing a studio with the successful mural painter Edward Holslag in the prestigious Tree Studios building on the Near North Side, and he joined the Palette and Chisel Club, where many members shared his background in illustration work.[33] That summer, he accompanied Holslag on a painting trip to Gloucester, Massachusetts, possibly also visiting nearby Rockport as well as Vermont.[34] With Eugenie he traveled to Sioux City, Iowa, their destination for collie business two years earlier.[35] Adding the Midwestern landscape to his growing fund of subjects, in 1920 he participated in a show of canvases inspired by the Cook County Forest Preserve, then enjoying particular attention as a setting for landscape painting.[36]

In June 1920 Aldrich and Eugenie departed for a seven-month trip to Europe, intending to travel in France, Italy, Belgium, Holland, and Great Britain.[37] Their actual itinerary is unknown, and the paintings that supposedly resulted only underscore the problematic nature of Aldrich's production as biographical documentation. Several versions of his view of the famous Pont Fleuri in the Breton town of Quimperlé (Plate 12) are dated 1921, after his return to the United States, thus testifying to his practice of painting from sketches, from memory, and possibly by simply copying earlier works – his own as well as Thaulow's. Following the practice of many illustrators, including fellow members of the Palette and Chisel Club, Aldrich developed a stylized monogram, with which he often marked the backs of his paintings in this period (Figure 1.4).

In the years following his return from abroad, Aldrich exhibited his recent paintings of France in Sioux Falls, South Dakota, returned to Davenport's Tri-City Art League for a solo show, and debuted in South Bend, Indiana, and in Aurora, Illinois.[38] In these and other prosperous Midwestern manufacturing cities, he found enthusiastic patronage from members of a growing class of managerial workers eager to acquire the signs of cultivation as well as affluence. In the booming postwar period many were settling into spacious historical-revival-style houses in newly developed subdivisions and becoming active in civic affairs; often their wives were members of art associations and women's clubs, such as South Bend's Progress Club, that were directly concerned with bringing high

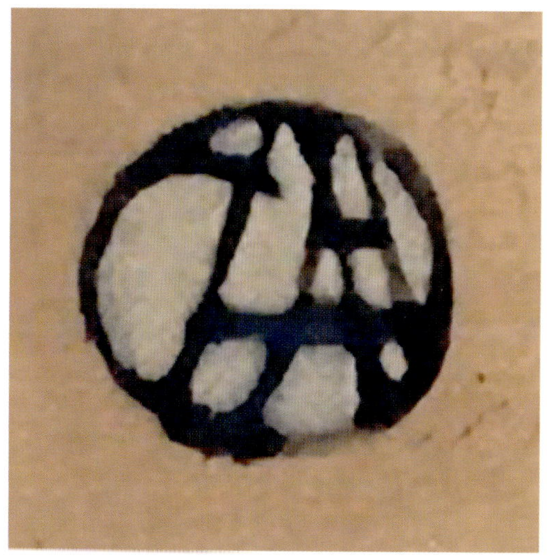

1.4. Aldrich's monogram inscribed on the verso of *The Chaumière, River Elaune,* ca. 1925. Photograph courtesy of Mario A. Mirelez and Eckert & Ross Fine Art, Indianapolis.

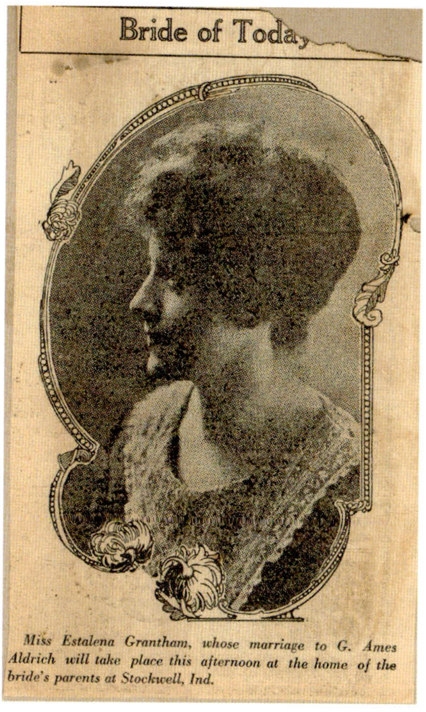

Bride of Toda[y]

Miss Estalena Grantham, whose marriage to G. Ames Aldrich will take place this afternoon at the home of the bride's parents at Stockwell, Ind.

1.5. Esta Grantham, from a marriage notice in an unidentified newspaper, December 24, 1922, in the artist's scrapbook. Collection of Peter Lundberg, Janus Galleries, Madison, Wisconsin. Photograph courtesy of Peter Lundberg, Janus Galleries.

culture to the local community. Aldrich's romantic images of a vanished Old World or of the beauties of native scenery suited their conservative idea of art, flattered their social aspirations, and harmonized with the consciously tasteful decor of their homes. Where his art was on view, the artist himself often was a conspicuous presence. Assiduously cultivating the local press, he was lionized as "one of America's best-known artists," a distinguished painter with an international reputation – one largely of his own invention.[39]

Aldrich may have arrived in the Midwest with a particular connection to Indiana, for one of his associates during his student days in Paris was Brandt Steele (son of Hoosier landscape painter T. C. Steele), who in the 1910s became a member of the lively Arts and Crafts movement in Indianapolis.[40] Aldrich had a solo gallery show there in 1923, but he focused his attention instead on South Bend.[41] It offered not only the advantage of commuting distance to Chicago but also the promising combination of a dearth of resident professional artists and a hunger for art among a prosperous middle class.[42] Following his 1922 debut with a generous display at the Oliver Hotel, he was represented in the Progress Club's annual art display of 1923 by fifty paintings and the next year received a solo exhibition at the South Bend Woman's Club.[43]

Aldrich quickly put down roots in South Bend, if only temporary ones. He and Eugenie had parted ways sometime after their return from Europe in early 1921, and at the end of 1922 he married South Bend resident Estalena (Esta) Grantham, a schoolteacher, graduate of Indiana University, and member of the Progress Club (Figure 1.5).[44] The couple's only child, Elizabeth (Betty), was born in 1924. Taking up residence in the city, Aldrich became perhaps its most prominent representative of the professional artist type. He founded the Fine Arts Club, where he gave instruction in landscape painting, etching, and theatrical design, and he wrote occasional columns for the *South Bend Tribune*.[45] He also traveled frequently, spending the summer of 1924, for example, painting in Gloucester.[46] Perhaps anticipating that he would exhaust the market in South Bend, where he had made a significant number of sales, he cultivated a new public in Aurora with an important show there in 1924.[47] In 1926 he exhibited with

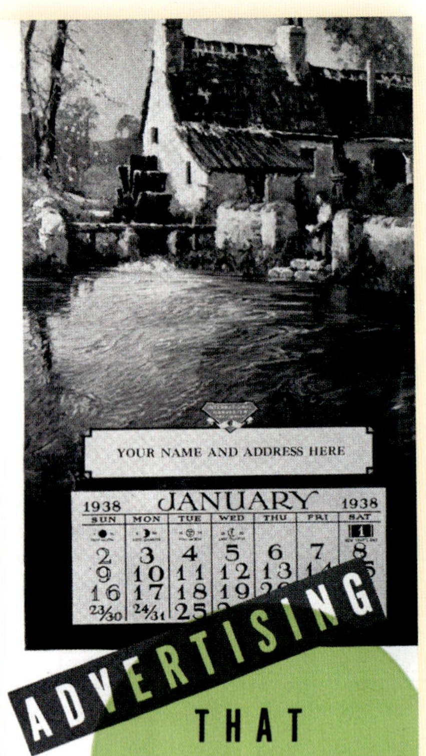

1.6. Notice for a promotional calendar featuring Aldrich's *A Bit of Old Normandy*, from *Harvester World* 28 (July–August 1937), 18. McCormick-International Harvester Collection, Wisconsin Historical Society, Madison, Wisconsin, image 90900.

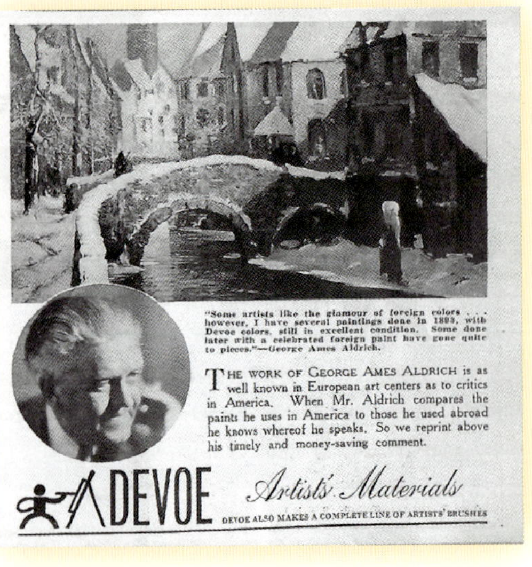

1.7. Advertisement for Devoe Artists' Materials in *Arts Digest* 10 (June 1, 1936), 19.

honors in the Richmond Art Association's annual show and he was represented in group exhibitions in Davenport, Fort Wayne, and Rockford, and made a much-publicized return visit to Rock Island.[48]

In the mid-1920s Aldrich was at the height of his professional success. He renewed his activities in Chicago, joining the newly formed Hoosier Salon and Chicago Galleries Association while continuing to exhibit in the Art Institute's *Chicago and Vicinity* annual. He won awards at each, and in 1927 he was featured along with fellow Palette and Chisel Club members Oskar Gross and Edward T. Grigware in a special exhibition at the Chicago Galleries Association, garnering his only significant notice in the Chicago press.[49] He also made an attempt at greater national exposure. In 1926 one of his prize-winning paintings was juried into the Sesquicentennial International Exposition in Philadelphia, and he submitted another (unsuccessfully) for that year's Carnegie International exhibition.[50] Aldrich took a rather scattershot approach to institutional affiliation. Over the years he participated in isolated exhibitions with such organizations as the Chicago Society of

Artists (in 1920), the All-Illinois Society of Fine Arts (in 1926), the Association of Chicago Painters and Sculptors (in 1927), and the Arts Club of Chicago (in 1932), but he apparently contributed little to their institutional life. His most permanent connection was with the Hoosier Salon, where he received a series of honors that included major prizes in 1926, 1929, and 1932.[51]

As he took greater advantage of opportunities in Chicago, Aldrich moved back to the city's South Side in 1926 with his family.[52] He also continued his pattern of travel. In 1929 he made a solo final trip to Europe, of which his busy beach scene (Plate 51) is probably a souvenir, and in the early 1930s Esta and Betty accompanied him on repeated summer excursions to Jackson, Michigan, and Rochester, Minnesota.[53] Simultaneously Aldrich maintained a presence in Indiana, however. Spending extensive periods in and around South Bend, he continued to write his column for a local newspaper, very much in the tone of a proud South Bend citizen, and his last solo exhibition took place in Muncie, in 1932.[54] That summer, as he exhibited and painted at the Spink Hotel on Lake Wawasee, Indiana, he promoted his "Hoosier Summer School of Art," which never materialized.[55] It was yet another manifestation of a habit of energetic self-promotion that also resulted in the publication of one of his characteristic winter landscapes in the *Christian Science Monitor,* again in 1932.[56]

Aldrich maintained the public character of the internationally successful landscape painter, but even as he continued to exhibit and garner notice as a celebrated Hoosier artist he was leading a somewhat hand-to-mouth existence that occasionally reduced him to using poor-quality materials (including house paint), bartering his paintings for necessities, and even going house-to-house in South Bend to sell his canvases.[57] A victim of alcoholism and depression, he was treated with indulgent understanding by South Bend–area acquaintances such as Theodora Makielski, owner with her husband, Joseph, of a local gallery and framing business, who would take him in as he recovered from spells of inebriation; eventually, he became a periodic inmate in a state psychiatric hospital in Elgin.[58] By the time the stock market crash heralded a sharp contraction of the art market in 1929, Esta had already returned to work as a public high school teacher to help support the family.[59] Until nearly the end of his life Aldrich continued to paint, turning out variations on his favorite themes, although evidence that he put earlier dates on some canvases suggests his own awareness that his best work was past.[60] After participating in a group show in Muncie in 1933, his exhibiting was limited to the Hoosier Salon.[61] Yet ever in pursuit of new opportunities for sales and exposure, he sold rights to several paintings to corporations, including Chicago's International Harvester, for use in promotional materials (Figure 1.6).

Aldrich died in his South Side Chicago home on March 7, 1941, at the age of sixty-eight. He left a legacy of an estimated one thousand landscape paintings, of which a large majority feature flowing streams in rural or pastoral settings.[62] A few years earlier, in a magazine advertisement for Devoe artists' materials, he once more assumed the image of an internationally renowned painter (Figure 1.7). His endorsement was accompanied by the pronouncement that "The work of GEORGE AMES ALDRICH is as well known in European art centers as to critics in America." The artist had certainly convinced the world that this was so, or at least his public in many Midwestern cities and towns. There, Aldrich found a niche for romantic images as fictional as his own public persona.

FROM MONTREUIL TO THE MIDWEST

ALDRICH'S ART IN CONTEXT

WENDY GREENHOUSE

The paintings of George Ames Aldrich reveal a romanticist. . . . [who] sees an idyll in a French village and a magnificent pageant in a steel foundry.

FADING DAYLIGHT ILLUMINATES THE SCENE FROM A high horizon. Rustic cottages or a tumbledown mill crowd an upper corner of the composition, perhaps with the unobtrusive figure of a woman standing by. Dominating the picture, above all else, is a swiftly flowing stream rendered with more careful attention than its surroundings. Edged by rounded banks formed by the tangled roots of bordering trees, the water's broken surface is deftly rendered in distinct strokes of the brush. The stream nearly fills the foreground and marks a deep diagonal recession toward distant fields and woods. The scene is overlaid with softening shadow; the mood is tranquil, with a hint of mystery. The only movement is in the water, but its perpetual flow underscores the impression of an unchanging remote world of tradition and timeworn habit.

This signature landscape formula sustained the prolific career of George Ames Aldrich for nearly forty years, and it continues to draw collectors with a taste for the pleasing mode known as decorative impressionism, widely practiced in the early decades of the twentieth century among conservative Midwestern landscape painters. Particularly after World War I, many of them focused on American subjects, but Aldrich's artistic identity remained closely tied to the French rural villages, cottages, mills, and streams that he had pictured since the beginning of his career as a landscape painter, in the first decade of the twentieth century. Known as a "wizard at painting running water and snow covered banks," he appears to have executed variations on this theme, with or without buildings, until nearly the end of his life, when his initial European sojourn was only a distant memory.[1] By then, an approach to landscape painting once regarded as modernist, emulated by Aldrich from the much-admired Norwegian painter Fritz Thaulow, had morphed into an embodiment of convention, a domesticated commodity well suited to the conservative cultural values of middle-class Midwesterners.

From the beginning, as demonstrated by *The River Elaune, Bellengreville* (Plate 4), one of the earliest of his rare dated canvases, Aldrich infused his European village landscapes with a mood of nostalgic retrospection. Ancient, humble rustic dwellings, weighted under hipped thatched or tiled roofs, wear an air of picturesque neglect. Rounded and shadowed as if by

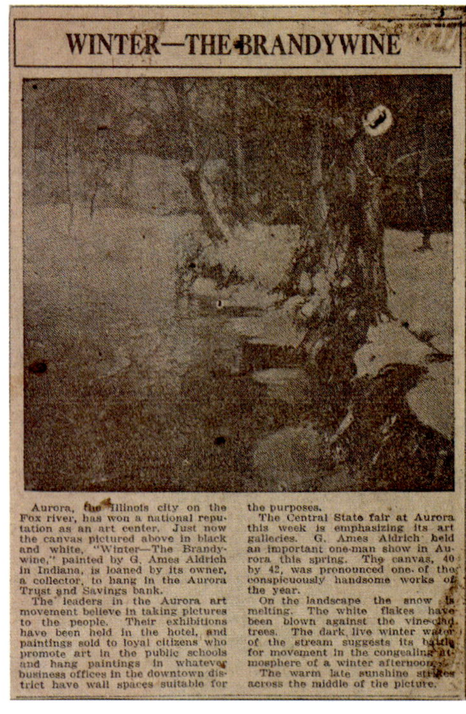

WINTER—THE BRANDYWINE

Aurora, the Illinois city on the Fox river, has won a national reputation as an art center. Just now the canvas pictured above in black and white, "Winter—The Brandywine," painted by G. Ames Aldrich in Indiana, is loaned by its owner, a collector, to hang in the Aurora Trust and Savings bank.

The leaders in the Aurora art movement believe in taking pictures to the people. Their exhibitions have been held in the hotel, and paintings sold to loyal citizens who promote art in the public schools and hang paintings in whatever business offices in the downtown district have wall spaces suitable for the purposes.

The Central State fair at Aurora this week is emphasizing its art galleries. G. Ames Aldrich held an important one-man show in Aurora this spring. The canvas, 40 by 42, was pronounced one of the conspicuously handsome works of the year.

On the landscape the snow is melting. The white flakes have been blown against the vine-clad trees. The dark, live winter water of the stream suggests its battle for movement in the congealing atmosphere of a winter afternoon.

The warm late sunshine strikes across the middle of the picture.

2.1. *Winter – The Brandywine,* reproduced in an unidentified newspaper, from a clipping in Aldrich's scrapbook. Collection of Peter Lundberg, Janus Galleries, Madison, Wisconsin.

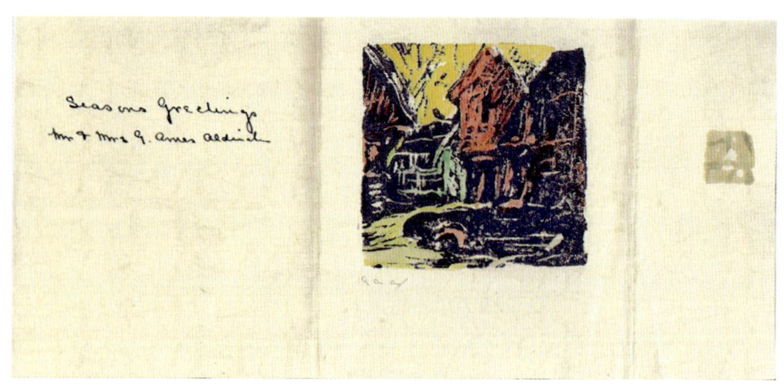

2.2. Aldrich's holiday greeting card, date unknown. Woodblock print, 5 × 10 inches. Collection of Peter Lundberg, Janus Galleries, Madison, Wisconsin.

the wearing of time, river banks and buildings seem virtually fused by a veil of shadows, by trailing vines and foliage, or by unified color tonalities, suggesting a time-honored harmony of man and nature, but never the privations of rural life and the hardships of physical labor. Combining romantic scenery, elegiac sentiment, and facile technique, Aldrich's typical paintings offer comfort laced with a touch of melancholy and regret. They promise a dreamy respite from quotidian reality and modernity, delivered in a formula that seems to have been remarkably winning, for Aldrich's broad public eventually extended from numerous private collectors to publishers of mass-market reproductions. Only the artist's alcoholism, later compounded by the market strictures of the Great Depression, could derail a career founded on so sure a recipe for success.

VARIETIES OF ARTFUL EUPHEMISM: ALDRICH AND THE DECORATIVE LANDSCAPE

Over a period of some thirty years, Aldrich made innumerable iterations of his formula composition of a stream flowing past rural buildings. His titles claim for them a variety of settings in rural northwestern France, including Bellengreville, Montreuil, Pernois, and Pont Aven. With subtle changes to or the elimination of background buildings, he shifted his setting to northern Indiana or Illinois, the Canche, Elaune, or Aven rivers becoming Juday Creek, the St. Joseph, the Kankakee, or the fanciful "Brandywine" (Plate 25, 26; Figure 2.1).[2] At least as measured by auction records, "typical Aldrich" river landscapes account for a staggering proportion of the artist's uncounted total oeuvre, which may run to more than a thousand paintings.[3] Yet as demonstrated in the selection in this publication, he painted a range of subjects far greater than those found in northern France and Holland. These include coastal Massachusetts (Plate 31) and perhaps Maine (Plate 34), the mountains near Rutland, Vermont (Plate 29), the Dakota Badlands (Plate 38), and New Mexico (Plate 39). His Midwestern subjects embrace both rural and industrial Indiana and Illinois (Plate 28, 41, 45), extending even to Chicago's steel mills and skyline (Plate 44, 46), but he also executed idealized pastoral landscapes of pure fantasy, in murals as well as easel paintings (Plate 10). He essayed multi-figural images and single-figure studies, in addition to floral still lifes (Plate 52). Aldrich is also said to have made commissioned portraits, "paintings of the negro cabins as viewed in Alabama," and even, in the early 1930s, some now-unidentified "modernistic pictures."[4] And he created both figural and landscape images in the print medium of etching.

Aldrich's paintings vary in style as well as subject. His fresh oil-on-board sketches (Plate 14, 27) are evidence of plein-air practice, and his distant view of a European church (Plate 13) is an objective study of the effect of sunset's stark illumination on bulky geometric forms and their color. These works evince an awareness of Impressionist style and practice quite set aside in more typical paintings, from his dreamy Tonalist views of Gloucester harbor (Plate 31) to his color-saturated moonlit nocturnes, with their story-book romanticism (Plate 21, 22, 23). An aerial image of village rooftops (Plate 15), with its patterned brushwork, strong color contrasts, and dramatically tipped-up perspective, approaches a modernist distortion more fully explored in a small expressionist woodblock print image created for an undated holiday greeting card (Figure 2.2). He painted a quarry works in an uncharacteristically factual manner that suggests in style as well as subject the realism of American Scene painting (Plate 45), but applied to another industrial scene (Plate 41), possibly Mishawaka's Ball-Band plant, the romanticism of his imaginary Arcadias (Plate 49). Such contrasts may well represent overlapping phases of what was evidently a high-volume painting practice. Its chronology may never be firmly established, for as well as continually revisiting favorite subjects and themes, Aldrich rarely dated his innumerable, often interchangeably titled canvases.

Some of Aldrich's habitual techniques and motifs – rich, rather fanciful color, square or nearly square canvas proportions, dramatically high (or, in rare cases, low) horizons, patterned brushwork, and deep spatial recession – are common to much of the so-called decorative landscape painting of the late 1910s and the 1920s. Like fellow Chicago-area contemporaries Carl Krafft (Figure 2.3) and Frank Peyraud (Figure 2.4), among others, Aldrich harnessed such features for comforting emotional as well as formal effect. These artists created an art of harmonious color and balanced composition, aimed at pleasing if not inspiring, offering a satisfying aesthetic experience of wholeness, resolution, and repose. Their works were decorative not just in a formal sense confined to their function as autonomous aesthetic objects but also in a conscious relationship to the domestic settings for which they were ultimately destined. In an era when pictures were increasingly "bought to suit decorations," conservative landscape painters in particular aligned their productions with current standards of "good taste" in decor, defined by principles of unity, harmony, balance, and genteel propriety.[5]

Aldrich's individual approach to decorative landscape is characterized by a peculiar effect of languid weightedness. His buildings are ponderous volumes complemented by static, invariably faceless figures that may humanize but do not animate his compositions. In many of his works, a kind of legato grace of continuous, flowing line subtly unites the contours of disparate forms and unifies the painting surface; his Indiana woodlands, for example, are freighted with the drooping elegance of vine-laden trees. In his French river images, similar effects underscore a mood of a romantic association, a pleasurable regret for an imagined past. Blurred and softened, thinly screened by tree trunks, and cropped and compressed into the upper corners of his compositions, the rounded forms of cottages and mills appear as rooted outgrowths from a vanished timeless world – as Aldrich's American viewers might nostalgically imagine it in the wake of the Great War.

Aldrich's take on rural France reflects the evolution in the American artistic encounter with European rural existence away from the naturalistic portrayal of peasant life popular in the 1880s and 1890s to the poetic interpretation of its physical setting through the unified, shadowy tones and contemplative mood of the movement known as Tonalism.[6] When Aldrich began painting landscapes at Montreuil-sur-Mer, around 1904, the town was the adopted home of American painter Henry Golden Dearth, who applied a Tonalist approach to the local setting in his *Old Church at Montreuil* (Figure 2.5). Aldrich's early encounter with similar pictorial values is evident in *Le Soir, River Elaune* (Plate 2), one of his many French

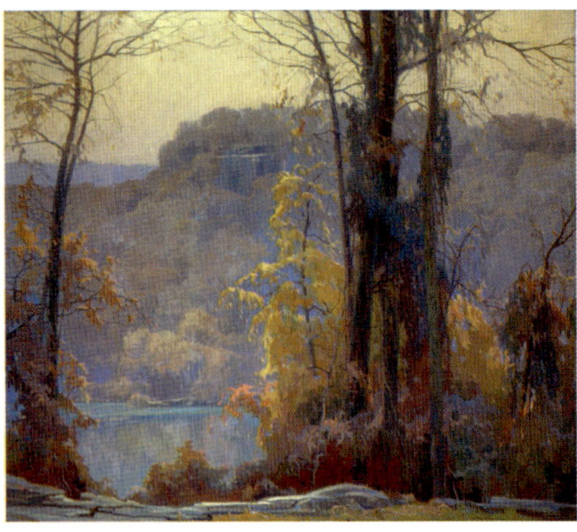

2.3. Carl R. Krafft, *Banks of the Gasconade,* 1920. Oil on canvas, 45 × 50 inches. Collection of the Union League Club of Chicago, UL1976.33.

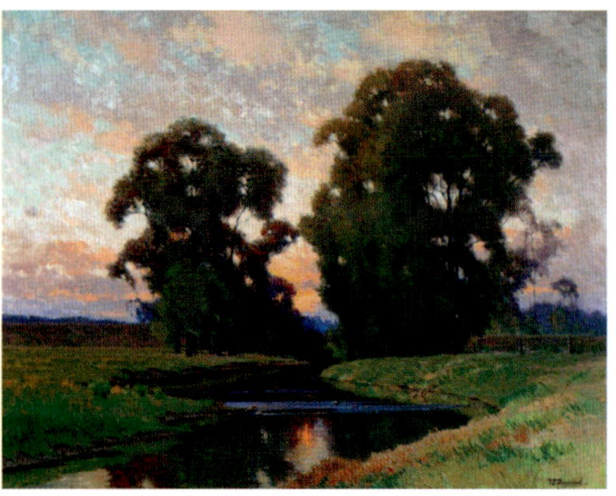

2.4. Frank C. Peyraud, *Summer Evening,* ca. 1927. Oil on canvas, 40 1/4 × 50 15/16 inches. The M. Christine Schwartz Collection, Chicago, Illinois.

rural views showing twilight or moonrise conditions and their attendant shadows and pastel tints.

Aldrich cultivated the fiction of a home in Montreuil well after the fact.[7] Whether this reflects his genuine personal nostalgia for the rural France of his early fine art career or his appreciation for the professional prestige of a European address in the eyes of American viewers, he continued to draw on his connection to the Old World not only for subjects but as the inspiration for an art of reverie, elegy, and unreality. His idyll of a bygone rural Europe was as remote and imaginary as his highly idealized, fantasy-like landscape vistas. In one example (Plate 47), a hazy softening of forms and colors interposes a scrim of unreality on an idyllic scene possibly inspired by an actual setting. Other images, such as the fancifully titled *Normandy Landscape* (Plate 48) and the summer-fall mural for the Oliver Hotel (Plate 49), appear to have a completely imaginary basis. The dreamlike quality of these visions of pure landscape beauty draws on the stylized decorative aesthetic of Arts and Crafts design; their air of stagey artificiality and their compositions' emphatic framing of distant vistas additionally recall Aldrich's early involvement in theatrical set design, a subject in which he later offered instruction to members of South Bend's Fine Arts Club. With the insertion of female figures in vaguely historical dress, as in *Indian Summer* (Plate 10), Aldrich additionally conjured a Continental tradition of gracious fête-galante imagery consistent with the fashionable historical revivalism of the 1910s and 1920s and already popularized in the paintings of California artist Frederick Ballard Williams. Like Aldrich, his Chicago contemporary Frederick Milton Grant, among other artists, was inspired to combine a Watteauesque theme and recognizably up-to-date painterly effects (Figure 2.6). Such works reflect the same deeply antimodern spirit that manifested itself in contemporary architecture and interior design in a renewed emphasis on a romanticized past – especially one sourced in Old Europe and Old New England – as a wellspring of stylistic reference and escapist fantasy.[8]

Outside France and the Midwest, Aldrich's most important single source of subjects was a similarly time-honored one: coastal Massachusetts, particularly Rockport and

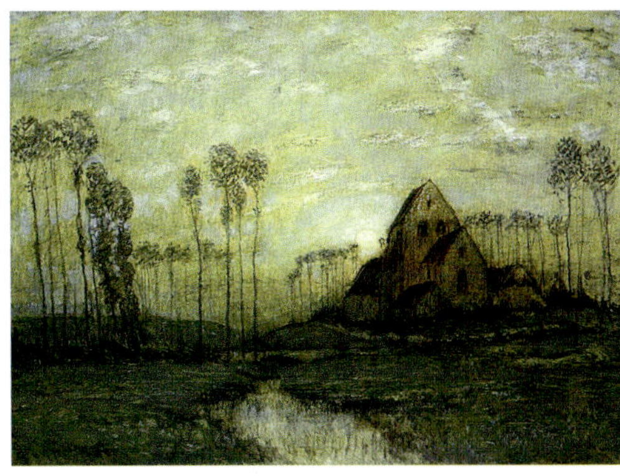

2.5. Henry Golden Dearth, *An Old Church at Montreuil,* ca. 1906–7. Oil on canvas, 36 3/8 × 47 1/2 inches. Smithsonian American Art Museum, Washington, D.C., gift of William T. Evans, 1909.7.17.

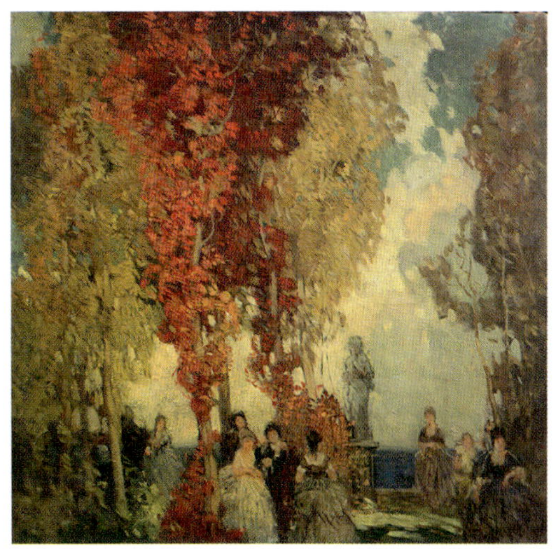

2.6. Frederick Milton Grant, *Figures in a Landscape,* undated. Oil on canvas, 30 × 30 inches. Courtesy of Spanierman Gallery, New York.

Gloucester, where by the early twentieth century quaintness was virtually an industry.[9] Often overlooking the industrial reality of these old fishing towns, artists long had pictured them as remnants of a more innocent America. Aldrich hints at this approach in his casual back-yard image of Sandwich rendered in a restrained Impressionist manner (Plate 30). As he painted the familiar subjects of the shipyards and harbor vistas of Gloucester and Rockport, however, he more typically imposed an extra note of nostalgic retrospection, using some of the formal techniques he had honed in the painting of French village scenes. In his view of the water from the hills of East Gloucester (Plate 31), for example, activity is muted and buildings reduced to silhouettes by the subdued glare of sun as it penetrates a haze of smoke, tinting distant forms a range of dreamy pastel hues. Possibly a late work created from distant memory, his painting of a shoreline crowded with a beached boat, drying sails, and shabby fishing shacks (Plate 33) is weighted with the prominent sag of suspended cables – not unlike the drooping vines and foliage common in his river landscapes – and an overall encrustation of small dabs of paint mimicking the curling of weathered shingle. In its high-keyed tints, his fresher *Gloucester Docks* (Figure 2.7) pays tribute to the crystalline light of morning in coastal New England, but the static backdrop of buildings, with their seemingly blank windows and closed doorways, emphasizes Gloucester's familiar identity as a place frozen in the past. The artificial stillness of this image, despite the figure in the foreground, is all the more evident in contrast to the breezy freshness animating the vigorously painted *Gloucester Harbor* by Aldrich's friend Edward Holslag (Figure 2.8).[10]

Aldrich approached even quite specific, local subjects with a corresponding circumspection. Finding Chicago a "depressing" subject for painting, he came no closer to it pictorially than in his evening view of the silhouetted skyline from the harbor (Plate 46).[11] Like the factories along Indiana's St. Joseph River (Plate 41), the modern city was best muted by distance and glimpsed from across his signature rippling waters. Settings for labor and activity shown close up, such as a boatyard (Plate 32), the quarry works (Plate 45), or archaic mills and factories along French streams (Plate 24), appear

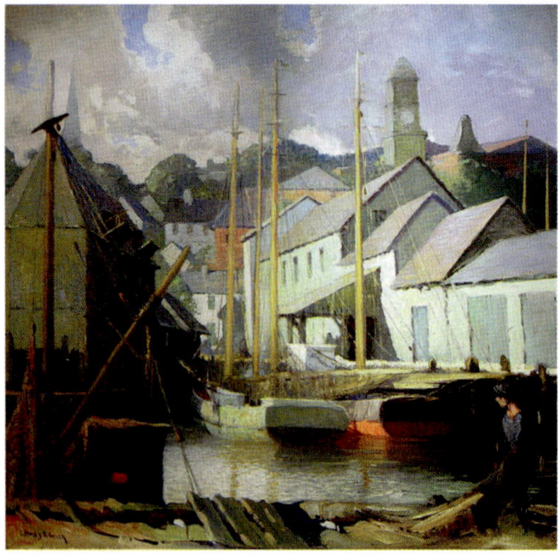

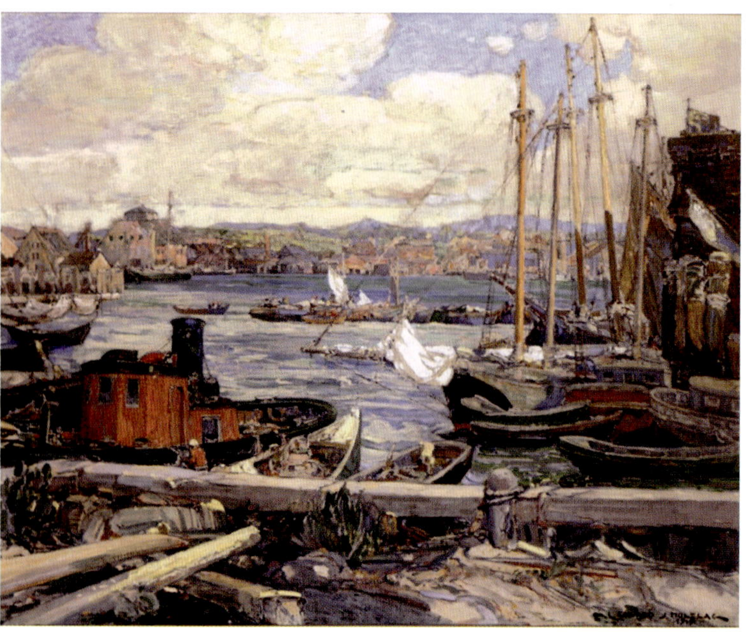

2.7. *Gloucester Docks,* undated. Oil on Masonite, 48 × 48 inches. Courtesy of Blue Heron Fine Art, Cohasset, Massachusetts.

2.8. Edward Holslag, *Gloucester Harbor,* 1919. Oil on canvas, 5 × 6 feet. Courtesy of Hirschl & Adler Galleries, New York.

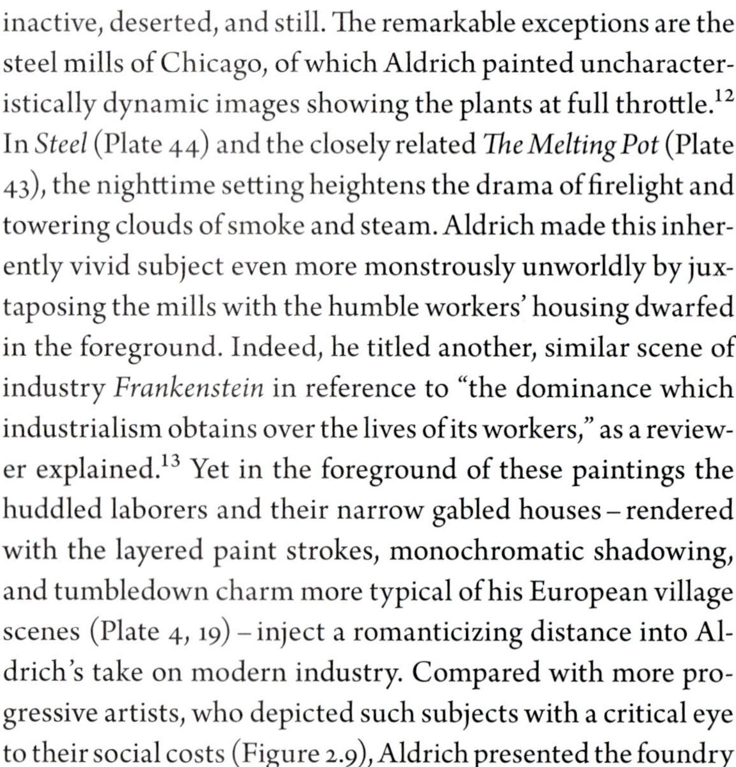

inactive, deserted, and still. The remarkable exceptions are the steel mills of Chicago, of which Aldrich painted uncharacteristically dynamic images showing the plants at full throttle.[12] In *Steel* (Plate 44) and the closely related *The Melting Pot* (Plate 43), the nighttime setting heightens the drama of firelight and towering clouds of smoke and steam. Aldrich made this inherently vivid subject even more monstrously unworldly by juxtaposing the mills with the humble workers' housing dwarfed in the foreground. Indeed, he titled another, similar scene of industry *Frankenstein* in reference to "the dominance which industrialism obtains over the lives of its workers," as a reviewer explained.[13] Yet in the foreground of these paintings the huddled laborers and their narrow gabled houses – rendered with the layered paint strokes, monochromatic shadowing, and tumbledown charm more typical of his European village scenes (Plate 4, 19) – inject a romanticizing distance into Aldrich's take on modern industry. Compared with more progressive artists, who depicted such subjects with a critical eye to their social costs (Figure 2.9), Aldrich presented the foundry as "a magnificent pageant" that amounts to a paean to modern industry.[14] Accordingly, *Steel* won the Hoosier Salon's Downs Prize, funded by the president of the Illinois Central Railroad to recognize the best industrial scene painted along its route.[15] Isolating the "picturesque" aspects of the steel mills, Aldrich, noted an approving reviewer, invested them "with color and light from his own fancy."[16] He thus brought even the strikingly modern theme of heavy industry in line with the artful euphemism of his more typical landscape imagery.

CONSTRUCTING A CAREER: ALDRICH, THAULOW, AND CHICAGO

Something of the willed fictionalization and romanticization of Aldrich's take on modern industry and rural life alike attends the shadowy career of the artist. He told numerous interviewers that he studied architecture at the Massachusetts Institute of Technology, exhibited at the Paris Salon as a member of the Société des Artistes Français, and spent somewhere

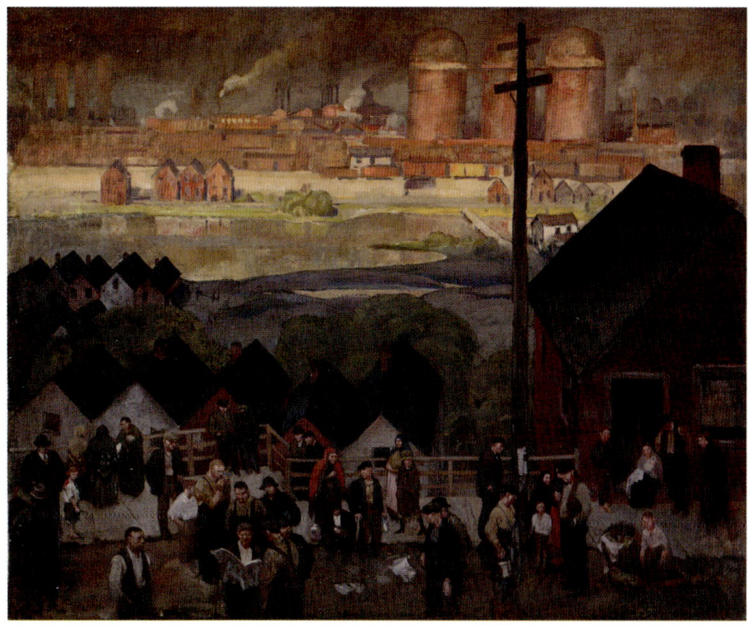

2.9. John Warner Norton, *Light and Shadow,* ca. 1924. Oil on canvas, 35 ½ × 41 ½ inches. The Art Institute of Chicago, Friends of American Art Collection, 1924.953. Photography © The Art Institute of Chicago

between eighteen and thirty years abroad, but these and other often-repeated "facts" are unsubstantiated and suspect, if not patently false.[17] They were evidently part of the fabricated identity as an internationally prominent artist with which Aldrich emerged from relative artistic obscurity in the late 1910s, when he arrived on Chicago's art scene, already in his mid-forties. Although a small number of paintings and prints, as well as a few sketches, can be dated to before that point, Aldrich's early activities as a fine artist are little documented. Yet he arrived in the Midwest an "eminent American artist" with an "international reputation as a painter of water," equipped with an impressive if unverifiable professional pedigree that provincial admirers of his paintings were apparently ready to accept at face value.[18] In fact, the Art Institute of Chicago's *Chicago and Vicinity* annual salon of 1918 is the earliest major fine art exhibition at home or abroad in which Aldrich is known to have participated. His career thereafter remained firmly anchored in the Midwest, although he traveled throughout the United States and made two return trips overseas. Aldrich was represented in only one known national exhibition outside his adopted home region, the 1926 Sesquicentennial Exposition in Philadelphia.[19]

There is no disputing the single most important fact about Aldrich's landscape painting: its indebtedness to Fritz Thaulow, particularly the images of streams flowing swiftly past humble rural dwellings for which the Norwegian artist remains best known. Aldrich's forthright adoption of Thaulow's compositional formula is demonstrated in any number of pairings of their works, such as his *Old Bridge at Pernois* (Plate 5) and Thaulow's *The Stream* (Figure 2.10). More particularly, Aldrich faithfully emulated Thaulow's celebrated treatment of the shifting surface of flowing water, using a loose facture that convincingly captures broken reflections and powerful currents. And he created other compositions that are almost disturbingly similar to individual Thaulow works. His vertical view of village rooftops (Plate 15) follows in essentials the layout and format of Thaulow's *Nocturne* (unlocated; Figure 2.11), for example, and the several versions of his *Washerwomen*

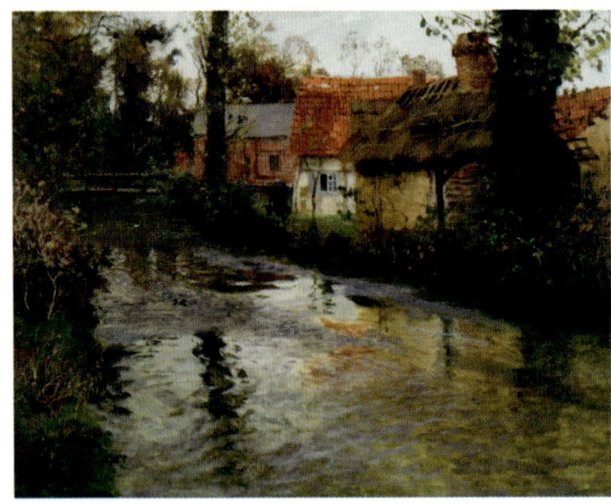

2.10. Fritz Thaulow, *The Stream,* ca. 1895. Oil on canvas, 23 ¾ × 28 ¾ inches. Memorial Art Gallery, University of Rochester, George Eastman Collection of the University of Rochester, 73.151.

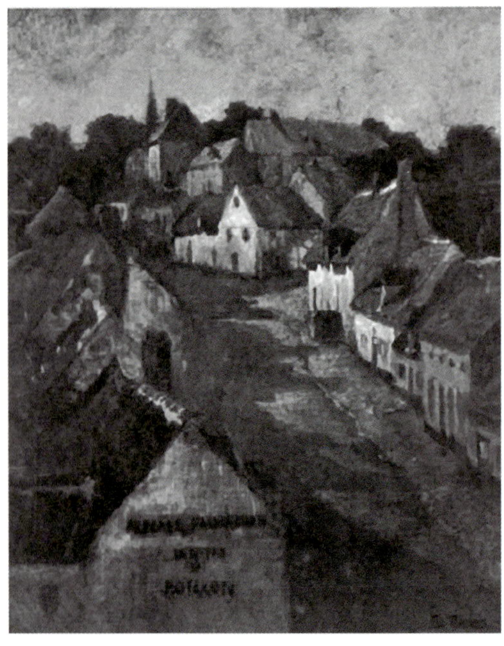

2.11. Fritz Thaulow, *Nocturne.* Unlocated painting reproduced in *The International Studio* 2 (July 1897), 3.

at Quimperlé (Plate 12) closely mirror Thaulow's very similar painting made two decades earlier (Figure 2.12); both Thaulow works were widely reproduced by the turn of the century.[20] For his own version, Aldrich could have used as a model one of several picture postcards of Quimperlé's famous Pont Fleuri, complete with laundresses (Figure 2.13). Yet he evidently followed Thaulow in modifying several industrial buildings in the background to give them a more domestic character, thus ensuring Quimperlé's image as an idyllic rural village.

When Aldrich arrived in Paris to study art in 1894, Thaulow's reputation was skyrocketing. One of the young American's reputed instructors, Jacques-Emil Blanche, was a close friend of Thaulow by at least 1895. Yet Aldrich would have needed no personal contact with the Norwegian to be exposed to his paintings, which were then circulating to great acclaim in Paris and beyond.[21] Aldrich was not the only American artist of his era to emulate Thaulow's subjects and techniques; the little-known Michigan painter Frederic Charles Vipond Ede was another. Aldrich was unique, however, in asserting a direct connection to the master, long maintaining that he had been Thaulow's favorite private pupil and painting companion during the last two years of the latter's life.[22] Much doubt has been thrown on such claims.[23] If not his pupil, however, Aldrich clearly studied Thaulow's compositions and technique firsthand, and he worked in several of the locales in northern France with which he was identified, notably Montreuil-sur-Mer. Aldrich arrived in the Midwest proclaiming himself the American successor to the famed painter, "whose themes he avows having chosen through preference and sentiment."[24] His snow scenes in the 1919 *Chicago and Vicinity* annual exhibition at the Art Institute were noted for "their refined Thaulow technique."[25] As a "pupil" of the admired artist, Aldrich successfully recast mere imitation as homage, making a virtue of emulation.

In the mid-1890s, Thaulow's works were being avidly purchased by several of America's most prominent contemporary art patrons, notably Henry Clay Frick, Andrew Mellon, and George Eastman.[26] They were equally admired by young members of an artistic avant-garde that included pioneering

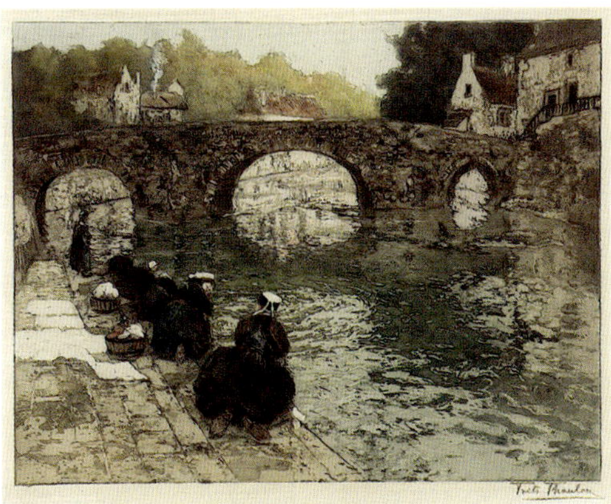

2.12. Fritz Thaulow, *Washerwomen at Quimperlé,* ca. 1902. Color aquatint after unlocated painting, 17 ¾ × 22 ⅞ inches.

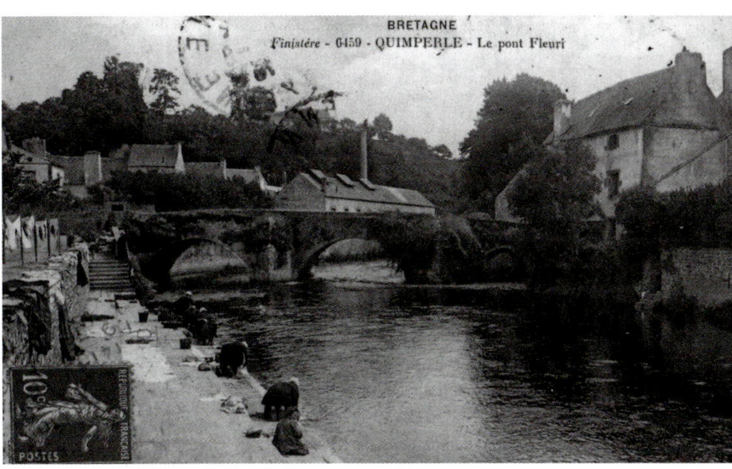

2.13. Picture postcard showing the Pont Fleuri, Quimperlé, Brittany (undated).

modernist photographers Alfred Stieglitz and Edward Steichen and the budding architect Frank Lloyd Wright, who decorated his own living room in suburban Chicago with a framed reproduction of Thaulow's celebrated *Thawing Ice* (or *Melting Snow*) of 1887.[27] Other Chicagoans shared their enthusiasm. In 1900, two Chicago dealers held separate exhibitions featuring Thaulow's paintings, and in 1903 a solo show of twenty-nine works at the Art Institute included many works from local private collections.[28] A major article on Thaulow appeared in the Chicago-based art journal *Brush and Pencil* in 1903, followed by another on the occasion of the artist's death three years later. By that date, the Art Institute itself owned two of his paintings and was exhibiting others from local private collections.[29] More than a decade after Thaulow's death, Chicago's longstanding admiration for his art may have influenced Aldrich to try his fortunes in that city and to persist in painting in a notably Thaulowesque manner. In perennially repeating a limited range of saleable compositions, Aldrich also was following the example of his master, who was said to have been forced by popular demand to continue painting the flowing water and snowy banks with which he had become closely associated.[30]

For his contemporaries, Thaulow's work represented one mode of emerging artistic modernism. His paintings' dramatic compositions, in which the horizon is crowded to the extreme upper limit above flowing water and stream banks, along with their broken brushwork and plein-air naturalism, appeared strikingly fresh and anti-academic. They exemplified a current trend in landscape painting at the turn of the twentieth century, the rejection of the full and finished "picture" in favor of "a scrap of Nature reproduced on the instant – just a momentary glimpse" that yet contained a keener "search after truth," in the words of one of the Norwegian's admirers.[31] Americans open to new developments in art yet still uncomfortable with the radical formal effects of artists such as Monet found in Thaulow's traditional rural and natural subject matter and his emphasis on poetic sentiment a *via media* between modernism and familiar pictorial values.

The artistic ground had shifted noticeably by the time Aldrich began promoting his Thaulowesque paintings among

Midwestern buyers in the post–World War I era. By then, Thaulow's modern synthesis of poetic affect and realist immediacy had evolved into something like a safe convention. In relation to more recent and far more radical approaches to art, a "sane" modernism, which could embrace rural imagery, was distinguished by such techniques as broken brushwork, the high horizon, disdain for detail and finish, and imaginative if harmonious color. Above all, it was marked by "little exaggeration, little overemphasis of an independent technique, [and] no striking of the supernote in coloring or in spirit."[32] Not only reliably representational, its unquestioning end remained the pleasing representation of something at once "real" and yet more picturesque, beautiful, or inspiring than any common reality. For most American art consumers as well as artists, the rectitude of this artistic ideal was only affirmed by the more recent developments in modernism that shocked and outraged many viewers of the International Exhibition of Modern Art – the so-called Armory Show – as it toured New York, Chicago, and Boston in 1913. By then, landscape painting dominated American exhibitions. But in the wake of the show, and as the outbreak of war overseas seemed to confirm the decadence of Europe, the "wholesome" portrayal of nature came fully into its own as a mainstream mode of artistic expression, its established purpose to "convey a mood rather than reproduce a scene," if not to provide an "inspirational influence."[33] Whether in the moody shadows of Tonalism or the vigorous brushwork and sunny color of Impressionism, its primary subject was nature domesticated – rural rather than wild, and moreover glimpsed in intimate fragments and quiet moments. Its exaltation of the commonplace, privileging of "atmosphere" over tangible fact, and emphasis on contemplative mood and personal experience invited the viewer to partake of the artist's subtle, cultivated vision, flattering his own sensitivity. Aldrich's romanticized images of an old Europe lost in time and now cut off by war seem calculated to embody an almost stereotypical genteel ideal of how art should look and how it should affect the viewer.

By the 1910s, the particular themes of receding stream and wintertime snow for which Thaulow was admired had attained the status of conventions in American landscape painting. John Twachtman had made a name for himself with his spare, elegant paintings of creeks in winter by the time Aldrich studied with him at New York's Art Students League in the early 1890s, and after the turn of the century such artists as Birge Harrison, Aldro Hibbard, Ernest Lawson, Edwin Redfield, and George Gardner Symons were noted for their own interpretations of this theme. In the Midwest, Frank Dudley, in his 1917 *Along the Creek* (Figure 2.14), and John Elwood Bundy, in *Winter Afternoon* (Figure 2.15), followed a familiar formula drawn from the picturesque local landscape. Audiences were conditioned to understand their quiet winter scenes as embodiments of refined sophistication in landscape art, cues for a personal engagement with "nature's moods" and an inspiration for poetic sensations. Aldrich's attachment to themes of pastoral nature in wintertime and the specific motif of the flowing stream put him in good company – and considerable competition – in the late 1910s and 1920s.

ALDRICH AND HIGH ART IN THE HEARTLAND

In his adopted city, Aldrich pursued a typical path to establishing himself on the local art scene. He successfully submitted works for the Art Institute's annual exhibitions, joined the prominent creative community in the Tree Studios building, and became a member of the congenial Palette and Chisel Club, many of whose members shared his background in illustration work. He responded to a crowded local field of landscape painting not only by associating himself with the revered Thaulow but also by developing a reputation outside Chicago, in smaller art centers. There, aspirations toward urban sophistication intersected with conservative cultural values, and a Parisian-trained professional artist cut a distinctive figure.

Aldrich's arrival in the Midwest coincided with the full flowering of an "art movement" that manifested itself in many heartland communities in the founding of art societies and in the activities of women's and civic organizations. In the reformist spirit of the era, their efforts were aimed at bringing high art and good taste into local settings through exhibitions, education programs, and the creation of public art collections that favored uncontroversial art, especially landscape

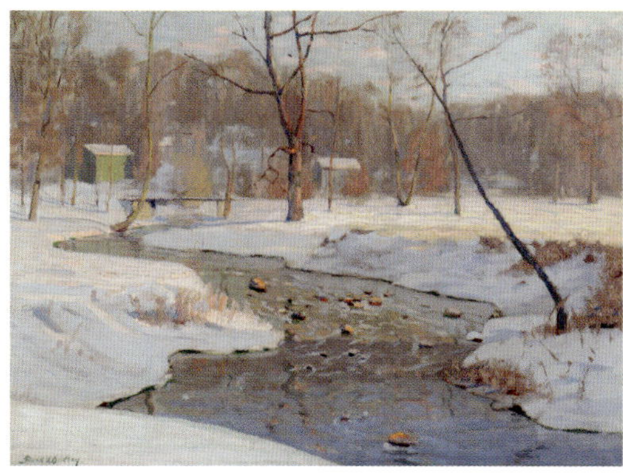

2.14. Frank V. Dudley, *Along the Creek*, 1917. Oil on canvas, 30 × 40 inches. Private collection.

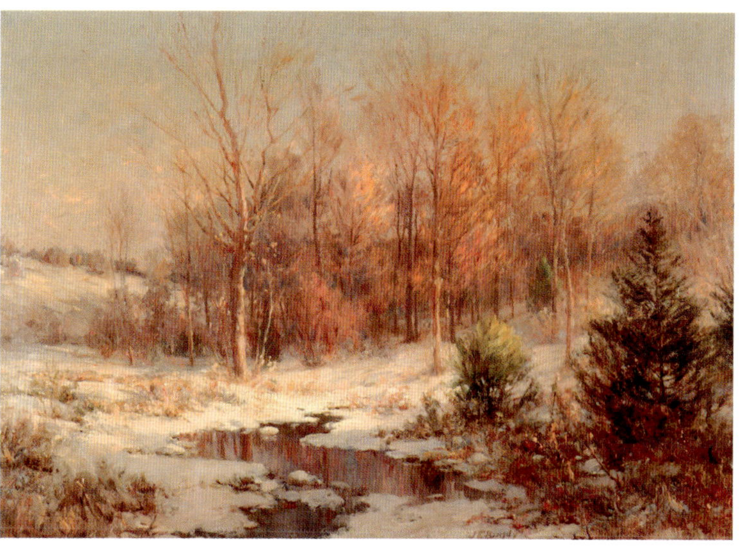

2.15. John Elwood Bundy, *Winter Afternoon*, ca. 1903. Oil on canvas, 25 × 30 inches. Haan Mansion, Lafayette, Indiana, Collection of Robert and Ellen Haan.

painting by regional artists.[34] Aldrich seems to have targeted this public from the beginning of the Midwestern phase of his career. His initial encounter with it in 1917 came through the Art Institute, whose Extension Department – then entering a period of particularly active and far-reaching activity in the hinterland – included one of his works in a selection of paintings by contemporary American artists sent for view at the Tri-City Art League in Davenport, Iowa, in 1917.[35] Over the next five years, Aldrich toured the region, holding solo exhibitions in Sioux Falls, South Dakota, and Davenport and visiting Rochester, Minnesota, as well.[36] His presence in Sioux City, Iowa, in 1919 vied for press attention with the local Fine Arts Society's recent purchase of his "famous" *Mill Pond* for an impressive $800.[37] In 1926, Davenport was again on his itinerary and his stay in nearby Rock Island duly reported.[38] In 1931, he sought to revive flagging sales with a solo exhibition at a Rapid City, South Dakota, hotel and a well-publicized return visit to Rochester.[39]

Since the beginning of his career in the United States, when he had placed paintings with a New York department store, Aldrich had gravitated toward venues that exposed a middlebrow public to his self-consciously "high" art. In Chicago his dealer was the high-volume J. W. Young Galleries, which promoted "art on a business basis," while in smaller markets his work was featured in "art shops" along with framing services, art supplies, and "decor."[40] In these and other accessible venues he met potential purchasers on their own terms. Women's clubs, art leagues, a chamber of commerce, and a college were among the bodies that sponsored exhibitions in which he participated or was featured. These took place in hotels, libraries, commercial galleries, private clubs, and a bank, in the absence of local art museums; in 1923 the artist staged a solo display of more than fifty paintings in his in-laws' church in the hamlet of Stockwell, Indiana.[41] Even in Detroit, home to a major art museum, Aldrich took his art to the people: by staging a solo show in a prestigious apartment building in 1928, he introduced his wares virtually into the homes of affluent potential buyers. His several trips to South Dakota seemed to have yielded more visibility and sales than paintings of its distinctive landscape.

Distinguished by a well-bred charm that echoed the style and subjects of his typical images, the artist himself was a notable presence in the many small towns and cities where his canvases were displayed.[42] Amidst a provincial art public, Aldrich appeared to advantage as an artist with an East Coast pedigree and a prestigious if exaggerated history of long residence in France, the "facts" of which were emphasized in admiring newspaper accounts. "The fact that he wears a smock, paint bedabbled, when he works, and has a mop of thick hair, proves that he is the artist of tradition," enthused the *Sioux City Daily Tribune*, apparently without irony.[43] In later years, he was known to wear a black cape, cultivating the image of the bohemian artist.[44]

Aldrich soon gravitated toward Indiana. He had a solo gallery show in Indianapolis in 1923, but he was already focused on South Bend, a vital regional manufacturing center where the growth of a corporate community dominated by such names as Studebaker, Oliver, Singer, and Bendix saw the corresponding development of a prosperous middle class. Aldrich debuted in South Bend in 1922 with a display of fifty-four works at the Oliver Hotel.[45] He married a South Bend native at year's end and took up residence in the city, living at various times at the Oliver Hotel and, in 1925, at the prestigious new Mar-Main Arms apartments, and painting murals in each.[46] His wife was a member of the art section of the Progress Club, a highly visible women's civic organization in South Bend, and in 1923 the artist shared center stage in the club's fourth annual art exhibition with landscape painter Alexis J. Fournier, another recent transplant to the city. In 1924, the South Bend Woman's Club gave Aldrich a solo exhibition.

South Bend was no stranger to artists. To accompany its 1921 art exhibition the Progress Club, for example, offered a program that included presentations by Lucie Hartrath, L. O. Griffith, Anna Lynch, Frank Dudley, and Pauline Palmer; a painting by Palmer was acquired that year for the club's collection. These mainstays of the Chicago art establishment were guests in South Bend; Aldrich, in contrast, put down roots in the city as both resident and working artist. Within a few months of his debut exhibition, he was at the center of the founding of a Fine Arts Club, a venue for his classes in color etching and theatrical design as well as landscape painting.[47] At the Progress Club exhibition, he gave demonstrations of his painting process and technique and hosted a reception for the husbands of club members.[48] Such activities undoubtedly lubricated many a sale, and his 1924 solo exhibition at the Woman's Club consisted mainly of works already owned by residents.[49] Effusive local newspaper coverage of the artist's activities carried a note of congratulatory self-consciousness of South Bend's artistic sophistication and discernment. After Aldrich officially moved back to Chicago, in 1926, he maintained strong ties to the city and spent much time in Indiana, as well as southern Michigan, painting, teaching, and exhibiting. Moreover, he continued to identify with the state by exhibiting almost every year in the Hoosier Salon, a Chicago venue for Indiana artists, notwithstanding his Chicago address.[50] In a column written for the *South Bend Tribune* around 1930, Aldrich referred to "my South Bend complex," a chip-on-the-shoulder attitude in relation to Chicago, and in 1933 he was included in an exhibition of paintings by Indiana artists in Muncie.[51] In 1932, Aldrich even proposed to found a "Hoosier Summer School of Art," a colony of artists and musicians with himself at its center.[52] His continued identification with South Bend in particular no doubt endeared him to locals, several of whom came to his aid when, periodically, drinking and money woes got the better of him.[53]

Aurora, Illinois, was another smaller art center where Aldrich made a calculated splash in the 1920s, and he claimed residence there briefly in 1926.[54] He found a vigorous champion in R. H. Conklin, an artist who ran a gallery out of his Aurora studio.[55] In 1924, Conklin arranged an exhibition for Aldrich – reportedly the city's most important one-man show to date – at the Aurora Chamber of Commerce, plugging it energetically in the local and national press.[56] *Art News* noted that resulting sales of nine paintings had brought in a total of $4,400 from buyers from several surrounding communities, and an Aurora newspaper trumpeted the fact that many of the paintings had found positions of honor in local homes.[57] Soon afterward, Conklin and his associate, Roy C. Haines, organized Aldrich's solo show at the South Bend Woman's Club, promoting it as evidence of the local citizenry's discerning taste, and Conklin probably was responsible for the illustration of Aldrich's painting *Winter* appearing in the September 1924 issue of the *American Magazine of Art*.[58] Reporting on a tour of central Indiana made with the artist, Conklin cited the Aldrich paintings he "happened" to find in many Indiana homes as proof that Hoosiers were waking from "their artistic lethargy," and he warned Illinoisans not to be upstaged. Just as Aldrich fulfilled expectations for the artistic "type" with his "paint-bedabbled smock" and "mop of thick hair," so his paintings might serve as a standard for fine art and their purchase a measure of personal and civic cultural arrival.

Although such efforts to promote the buying of art, and specifically of Aldrich's paintings, speak to the potential public in the Midwestern heartland, it also suggests challenges to establishing a culture of fine art consumption. Aldrich's South Bend buyers were successful, often self-made manufacturers, retailers, and professionals; although typically involved in civic affairs, they may have been newcomers to collecting original works of art as substantial as oil paintings. Often, however, their wives were members of the thriving women's organizations, such as South Bend's Progress Club and Woman's Club, that in many small cities represented the primary sponsor of art exhibitions and activities. Thus, the institutional setting for art life reinforced the stigmatization of art as a plaything of female leisure. Acknowledging the embarrassment of the male first-time purchaser of art "afraid that his morals and business standing would be questioned," Aldrich organized a "stag night" during his Progress Club exhibition to encourage men to view the art in the congenial atmosphere of a single-sex gathering. There was nothing "loose, effeminate, daffy or cuckoo in the appreciation of fine works of art or in the pleasure derived from possessing them," he argued.[59] An artist was comparable to any businessman, according to Aldrich, in that he simply created a product, in his case beauty. For those unmoved by the appeal of beauty for its own sake, Aldrich proposed that collecting art – his art, by implication – redeemed itself as a sound financial as well as aesthetic investment.[60]

Aldrich's subjects, moreover, were freighted with specific appeal for his regional audience. Like his images of the Ball-Band plant, his pictures of the beautiful, unspoiled Midwestern woodlands flattered local civic pride as they flatteringly presumed a sophisticated urbanite's privileged ideal of therapeutic nature. More particularly, his signature motif of the flowing stream may have resonated with citizens of towns such as Aurora and South Bend that had grown up around water-powered industry and transportation. Following the example of Thaulow, Aldrich painted old-fashioned industrial buildings, dams, and mills, as well as cottages, alongside French streams (Plate 24). Beyond their purely picturesque appeal, Aldrich's subjects emphasized the longstanding link between industry and riverways. Indeed, one man reportedly purchased an Aldrich painting of an old mill at a tannery in Normandy because he owned a tannery in Rockford.[61] The striking verisimilitude of Aldrich's flowing waters may have particularly satisfied a businessman's respect for fact, while the contrasting vagueness with which he rendered his stock buildings and figures downplayed any evocation of the less picturesque realities of the industrial workplace. A further remove was effected by the temporally and geographically remote setting of rural France or the purely spatial distance commanded in his painted views of the Ball-Band plant.

Aldrich's contemporaries equated such unvarying euphemism with more purely spiritual rewards. Aurora insurance executive and art collector James M. Cowan, who owned no fewer than ten canvases by Aldrich in the mid-1920s, demonstrated his belief in art as a tool of civic improvement by putting them on public display in downtown offices and businesses; the Aurora Trust and Savings Bank, it was noted, would be a more effective means of bringing the improving influence of art to the people than those exclusive institutions, museums.[62] No such display of art could take place "without accompanying uplift, vision and good thought going along with it."[63] In an implied reproof to the cryptic or repulsive character of much modernist art, Aldrich's paintings were often described as "livable pictures" that presented an ideal of the beautiful "which is generally [i.e., popularly] understood and appreciated." As visions of "things with which [people] would adorn their lives if they could follow their heart's desire," these charming interpretations of remote or idealized places would equally "enrich and ennoble the home environment"

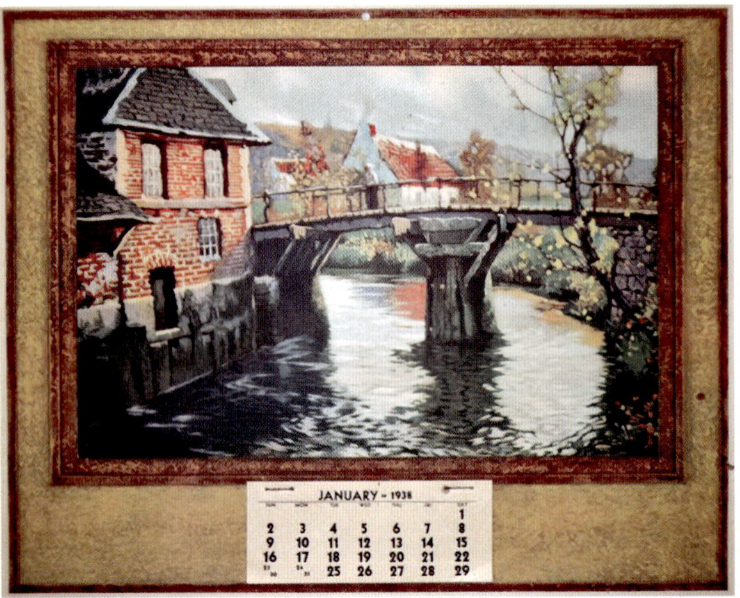

2.16. Calendar for 1938 issued by Caswell's National Crest Coffee, featuring Aldrich's painting *Springtime*. Collection of Peter Lundberg, Janus Galleries, Madison, Wisconsin.

or – on a more prosaic, material level – "any home interior."[64] Indeed, Aldrich's images of an idealized Old World or Old New England drew on an anti-urban nostalgia for an imagined past that was more tangibly expressed in the proliferation of period-revival-style homes in suburban subdivisions across 1920s America. Whether offering a nostalgic take on a bygone Europe or New England or a poetic celebration of heartland nature, an Aldrich landscape offered relief from "these days of breathless hurry."[65] International Harvester's promotional calendar for 1938 featured Aldrich's *A Bit of Old Normandy,* a romanticized idyll of rural life conspicuously remote from the mechanized agriculture promoted by the corporation. "Fast-moving Americans" contemplating a similar French mill scene by Aldrich on a coffee company's calendar for the same year (Figure 2.16) "soon respond to this atmosphere of restfulness, with its invitation to relax and just live" – presumably finding in it therapeutic relief from both the march of time and the stimulative effects of caffeine.[66]

Nowhere in America was more fast-moving than Chicago, but in 1926 Aldrich returned there at least part-time, while, as noted, retaining a close affiliation with South Bend. Perhaps his confidence in his competitiveness on the Chicago art scene was boosted by his winning the Thompson Prize in that year's *Chicago and Vicinity* exhibition at the Art Institute. Even as traditionalists such as Aldrich found themselves increasingly sidelined in a museum that was rapidly acclimating itself to modernism, they encountered alternate venues for exposure and sales. The mid-1920s saw the births of the Chicago Galleries Association, a commercial cooperative, and the Hoosier Salon, held in the galleries of the Marshall Field and Company department store.[67] Both offered direct access to "a large and many-minded public" of viewers not always comfortable with the modernist "isms" on display at the art museum or, for that matter, with the practice of owning original artworks; the CGA, for example, offered lay members the opportunity to borrow from a circulating collection of artist-members' work in an effort "to place 'art' in the hands of the public – to put it literally in the home."[68] While Aldrich continued to show almost annually in the Art Institute's *Chicago and Vicinity* exhibition through 1928, the CGA and especially the Hoosier

Salon, which kept his work visible to the Indiana public, became important outlets from which he carried off several awards and distinctions. The last was a winter landscape prize at the Hoosier Salon in 1932, a fitting final recognition of his status as the "wizard" of snow and streams.

In the final decade of his career, Aldrich made the ultimate connection to would-be art consumers he described as "not in the plutocratic class" – through the medium of mass-market reproductions.[69] In addition to the International Harvester and Caswell's Coffee calendars featuring French stream-and-mill paintings, these included a suitable-for-framing print of one of his signature Midwestern winter stream images (Plate 28): it was distributed to promote a popular brand of toothpaste, undoubtedly in the hope that viewers would associate the purity of Aldrich's snow with a brilliant smile. By then the hard-up artist, driven by alcoholism and depression to repeat stays in a state psychiatric hospital, could profit little from whatever windfall these reproductions brought. Yet such commercial applications of his work demonstrates the arrival of Aldrich's high art formula as a mass-market commodity, one that fulfilled a "generally understood" if only vaguely articulated notion of art as reliably representational, soothing in its harmonious effects, affirmative if not inspiring, and offering a decorous livability that would stand up to daily encounter.

In Aldrich's paintings, these qualities were most typically embodied in images that played to anti-modern anxiety in their romantic escapism, whether they presented such a quotidian subject as the modern factory or a European village-and-stream scene charged with wistful retrospection. Like Aldrich's largely fictive professional persona as an internationally renowned painter, his art was finely calibrated to ordinary Americans' conservative cultural values and aspirations to aesthetic sophistication. His individual paintings' rich tones, static and self-contained compositions, and bravura painterly effects underscored a quality of rarified singularity that he undermined, ironically, by prolific, even obsessive reiteration, as if acknowledging both the formulaic nature and the mass appeal of his images. Indeed, by the time Aldrich was promoting his art in the Midwest, its synthesis of precedent and convention was an accessible expression of a broad ideal of high art, if one distinguished by his individual brand of facile grace. Those conventions – from such material features as flowing streams, quaint cottages, and pristine snowy woods to the uplifting sentiment they were intended to inspire – have become entrenched in the popular construction of landscape art and in its mass-market manifestations. Pastoral nature, rendered in a traditional style and featuring a prominent body of water, remains the subject of "America's most wanted painting," according to a random survey conducted in the 1990s by the artistic team of Vitaly Komar and Alex Melamid.[70] So far the constructed narrative of American art has admitted little space to art that, like Aldrich's, conformed to artistic norms rather than contesting them, serving its immediate market rather than contributing to what may appear in hindsight an inexorable momentum of cultural progress. Like the shadows that round and soften Aldrich's signature rural images, the eclipse of the conservative cultural mainstream in historical memory may only obscure what was, and remains, solidly present. And for Aldrich's admirers of today, its values retain a surprisingly vital, if largely overlooked, currency.

NOTES

A BIOGRAPHY

Items from Aldrich's scrapbook of clippings and other ephemera in the collection of Peter Lundberg (hereafter "scr") are cited here by the unique page/item numbers assigned by Mr. Lundberg. For many of the newspaper clippings in the scrapbook, sources and publication dates are unknown.

1. Aldrich himself completed his 1894 and 1920 passport applications, which both give June 3, 1871, as the date of his birth. In the 1880 federal census record, he is listed as being ten years old, which supports the 1871 date. The date of June 3, 1872, noted on his 1915 passport may have been a clerical error, as the form was completed by another although signed by Aldrich. The 1872 date appears in most later sources, including the Illinois Death Index and the *Who Was Who in America* (Chicago: A. N. Marquis Company, 1943), 1:13. The information likely was supplied by his wife Esta. She may have believed 1872 to be correct, as that is the year recorded in their marriage license in 1922. The Cook County, Illinois, record of Aldrich's marriage to his first wife in 1919 gives "abt 1872" as his birth date. The census records, ship manifests, passport applications, and marriage and death records cited throughout are available on Ancestry.com.

2. United States Federal Census, 1880. Aldrich's mother's name is given as Caroline Elizabeth (Ames) Aldrich in the entry in *National Cyclopaedia of American Biography* (New York: James T. White and Company, 1944), 31:81.

3. *Who Was Who in America.*

4. The Art Students League's sketchy record of Aldrich's attendance indicates that he was enrolled from October 1891 to April 1892. Several accounts place him there in 1892–94.

5. Unidentified clipping fragment, scr 29/A7.

6. Janice H. Chadbourne, Karl Gabosh, and Charles O. Vogel, comps., *The Boston Art Club: Exhibition Record 1873–1909* (Madison, CT: Sound View Press, 1991).

7. Entitled *The Afternoon Tea,* his photograph was praised as "a picture that is unusually artistic." Henry Milford Steele, "The Artistic Side of Photography, with Illustrations Selected from Our Last Prize Competition," *The Quarterly Illustrator* 2 (July–September 1894): 326.

8. His 1894 passport application lists his intention to return to the United States "in ~~two~~ [*sic*] or three years." His 1920 application notes that he had previously lived in France between 1893 (i.e., 1894) and 1900.

9. Unidentified clipping, scr 63/A59.

10. Aldrich's other possible teachers include Kenyon Cox at the Art Students League; Jean-Paul Laurens and Jean Joseph Benjamin Constant at the Académie Julian; and Jacques-Emil Blanche and René François Xavier Prinet at the Académie Colarossi. All are noted in the undated brochure "The Art of G. Ames Aldrich" (unpaged, in Lundberg Aldrich files), a particularly inflated presentation of Aldrich's credentials, which internal evidence dates to around 1924. It was very probably the work of Aldrich's Aurora dealer, R. H. Conklin.

11. Two figural works, both studies of a solitary young woman in peasant dress, have passed through the art market in recent decades. An article in an Aurora newspaper in 1924 notes that Aldrich painted portraits in France before turning to landscape ("Another Art Exhibit Opens Here Tomorrow," *Aurora Beacon-News,* scr 32/A8).

12. The Académie Carmen operated only between late 1898 and early 1900, and Whistler's presence there was notoriously scarce. Many American artists in Paris claimed the coveted status of "pupil of Whistler" on dubious grounds. Stanley Weintraub, *Whistler: A Biography* (New York: Weybright and Talley, 1974), chapter 36; Robyn Asleson, "The Idol and His Apprentices: Whistler and the Académie Carmen in Paris" in Linda Merrill et al., *After Whistler: The Artist and His Influence on American*

Painting (New Haven and London: High Museum of Art and Yale University Press, 2003), 74–83.

13. Ibid., 444.

14. An AP obituary in an unidentified newspaper, "George Ames Aldrich, Landscape Artist, Dies," scr 48/A53, states that he began to work in illustration in 1899. According to *Who Was Who,* however, he ceased such work in 1899 to take up landscape painting. A few early drawings survive in Aldrich's papers (Lundberg Aldrich files), but no published illustrations have been identified and they may well have been uncredited. Aldrich is described, no doubt inflatedly, as being "one of the chief illustrators" for *Life* and *Truth* in "Art Society Buys Famous Painting," *Sioux City Daily Tribune,* July 8, 1919 (Lundberg Aldrich files). "Eminent Artist to Exhibit Here," scr 34/A15, refers to his work for *Life* and *Vogue.* The wide variation in accounts of his illustration work, all of which date to later in the artist's career, undermines confidence in their reliability.

15. "The Art of G. Ames Aldrich."

16. Moreover, as Thaulow expert Vidar Poulsson notes, he "did not really teach any French or American students his style of landscape painting" and he detested the imitations his popular work spawned. Poulsson suggests that Aldrich may have been responsible for some of the Thaulow forgeries still in circulation. Vidar Poulsson, email messages to Peter Lundberg, November 1 and 5, 2002, Lundberg Aldrich files.

17. On his 1920 passport application, he stated that he had lived in France for short periods between 1904 and 1910. Ship manifests record his return voyages to the United States in 1906, 1908, and 1910.

18. Aldrich listed Dieppe as his address in the 1909–10 edition of the *American Art Directory;* between 1919 and 1927, he listed Montreuil-sur-Mer as his home and various Chicago locales as his business address.

19. A Muncie, Indiana, newspaper, for example, was almost certainly quoting the artist when it proudly noted that during his years in France "his work attracted much attention and was hung in the [Paris] Salon and other continental exhibitions" ("George Ames Aldrich, Well Known Painter, Spending Week-end Here," unidentified Richmond, Indiana, newspaper, May 29, 1932, scr 34/A14). Aldrich is not listed among the members in the catalogues of the Société des Artistes Français; nor is there any information about him in its files (SAF president Viviane Guybet, email message to Wendy Greenhouse, August 19, 2011). According to Peter Lundberg, the few paintings by Aldrich that have appeared in European art auctions have American provenances. The artist always maintained that he was represented in the Musée de Rouen collection; however, no work of his is listed in the online Lafayette Database of works by U.S. artists in French national collections.

20. As George A. Aldrich he was listed among the pall bearers in "W. E. Marshall's Funeral," *New York Times,* September 2, 1906. Later Aldrich also claimed membership in the Mayflower Society, but this has not been verified.

21. According to the 1920 census, however, George and Eugenie were married in Paris in 1909. They were married again in Chicago on July 19, 1919, according to Cook County records. In the 1930 census, Aldrich reported that he had first been married at the age of 23 (that is, around 1894) – possibly the only corroboration of the statement in his entry in the *National Cyclopaedia of American Biography* that he had married three times. Eugenie's biography is as contradictory as her husband's. Census records and ship manifests give her birth date variously as 1879, 1888, and 1890 and her birthplace as either New York or Paris. For information on Eugenie Wehrle Aldrich, we are indebted to Susan Klein-Bagdad of Richard Norton Gallery, Chicago. See also Peter Hastings Falk, *Who Was Who in American Art 1574–1965: 400 Years of Artists in America* (Madison, CT: Sound View Press, 1999), 2:2455.

22. Three Aldrich paintings were illustrated in the women's section of the *New York Tribune,* April 7, 1907, with the note that James Rice, Jr., was to exhibit paintings by Geo. Ames Aldriche [*sic*] at his gallery at 14 John Street. Rice, a former diamond merchant who had begun collecting art for himself, left little additional record of activity as a dealer or gallerist. On Rice see Henry W. B. Howard, ed., *History of the City of Brooklyn from Its Settlement to the Present Time* (Brooklyn: Brooklyn Daily Eagle), 2:916. Gimbels department store advertisement, *Evening World,* April 22, 1912.

23. Aldrich returned alone from Boulogne in early 1908 and, accompanied by Mrs. Aldrich, from Rotterdam in late 1910. One George A. Aldrich traveled from San Francisco to New York via Panama in late 1911, but it has been impossible to identify him definitively with the artist.

24. *National Cyclopaedia of American Biography* gives New York as Aldrich's address in 1910. The record of Aldrich's patent on one of his paintings in 1911 lists Worcester. In 1914, Mrs. Aldrich launched her collie breeding activities in Philadelphia, as reported in *Dog Fancier* 23 (April 1914): 10, and *Dog Fancier* 24 (April 1915): 6. Aldrich's 1915 passport application gives Duxbury as his "permanent home."

25. On his theater designs, see "Players' Club Vodvil," *Altoona Mirror,* November 17, 1914. An undated clipping from a Mishawaka, Indiana, newspaper (scr 62/A56) claims that Aldrich had "handled scenic productions in New York and devoted considerable attention to this work while in France." Eugenie appeared on stage as "Mlle. D'Aures, the French actress" in Sioux City, where her husband had painted a drop curtain at the Orpheum Theater, according to "Art Society Buys Famous Painting," which notes that "in private life Mlle. D'Aures is Mrs. Aldrich." A Mme. D'Aures appeared in a vaudeville act at Chicago's State-Lake Theater in 1919, according to advertisements in *Chicago Tribune,* June 23, 24, and 26, 1919, but Eugenie's connection to her is unknown. In the 1920 census, Eugenie listed her occupation as dramatic actress. According to Library of Congress copyright records (available online), in 1909 Aldrich sold the rights to one of his paintings to the National Art Company, a commercial print and postcard publisher. He himself obtained patents on various works in 1910, 1911, and 1912. In 1916, one A. H. McQuilkin of Chicago took out a patent on an Aldrich painting.

26. Passport application, 1915; George Ames Aldrich, "Collie Notes by Amescroft," *Dog Fancier* 24 (December 1915): 12. In "Collie Notes from Mr. Aldrich," *Dog Fancier* 24 (November 1915): 13, Aldrich notes that he and his wife had been "pretty much all over the Pacific coast" in connection with dog breeding. Other columns report his visits to Winnipeg and Vancouver.

27. *Dog Fancier* 24 (November 1915): 13–14; 24 (December 1915): 12, 27; 25 (January 1916): 10, 28; 26 (March 1917): 11; 26 (July 1917): 12; 26 (August 1917): 10; 26 (October 1917): 29.

28. On the 1915 passport application, Aldrich's identity was vouched for by one John Suster of Des Plaines, who claimed six years' personal acquaintance with the artist. Amescroft Kennel's last advertisement in *Dog Fancier,* in October 1917, gives 6725 Stony Island Avenue, Chicago, as the address, which is also noted in Eugenie Aldrich's Art Institute enrollment record.

29. Ed Martin, "St. Louis Collie Club Show," *Dog Fancier* 25 (January 1916): 10; Geo. E. Dodd, "St. Louis Collie Club," *Dog Fancier* 26 (March 1917): 11; notice in *Dogdom* 17 (March 1918): 31. Any doubt that the collie breeder and the landscape painter were the same individual is removed by the description of Aldrich in the 1916 reference cited above: "While Mr. Aldrich is an ardent Collie

fancier, he is also a noted landscape artist, a pupil of Fritz Thaulow, Whistler, and the Academie Julienne [*sic*], Paris, and he has presented the club a beautiful painting of The River Arques (France)." He apparently never painted collies, however.

30. Evelyn Marie Stuart, "Public Palaces and Their Art Treasures," *Fine Arts Journal* 35 (October 1917): 47, illus. p. 41. Nathan M. Kaufman's acquisition of a reputed 700 paintings in 1915 is noted in his obituary in the *Chicago Tribune*, November 26, 1918.

31. Advertisement for Young's Art Galleries, *Chicago Tribune*, March 5, 1916; "Local Owners of Painters' Works," *Rock Island Union*, January 10, 1917.

32. An announcement in *Dog Fancier* (26 [October 1917]: 29) informed the public that Amescroft Kennels was selling off its entire stock. A note in the magazine the following March indicates that Aldrich was still breeding collies, if on a smaller scale (17 [March 1918]: 31).

33. Holslag served as president of the Palette and Chisel Club in 1919. A 1924 newspaper account states that he and Aldrich "worked shoulder to shoulder in establishing and building up" the club and made it "one of the leading art associations of the middlewest" ("Aldrich Exhibit Is Praised by Aurora Artist," scr 38/A32). This may well have been another of Aldrich's fictions, however, for in the club's records (Newberry Library, Chicago) he does not figure as an active member.

34. "Art Society Buys Famous Painting."

35. Ibid.

36. Eleanor Jewett, "Nature Studies Shown by Wild Flower Society," *Chicago Tribune*, January 11, 1920.

37. According to their passport applications, they planned to depart from New York in early June. A ship manifest documents their return in early January 1921.

38. "Artist Shows World's Beauty," unidentified Sioux City newspaper, scr 37/A24. The clipping notes that Aldrich had returned from France "last year" and had since been touring the country. "Noted Artist and His Family Guets [*sic*] of Mr. and Mrs. Swan at New Fort Armstrong Hotel" notes that at the Tri-City Art League hall in Davenport, "at one time an entire exhibit was his." Joel Dryer dates that solo exhibition to 1922.

39. "Organization for Study of Art Plan of Local Artists," scr 35/A18.

40. "Interesting Exhibit at Lieber's," scr 45/A45.

41. Ibid. The review notes that Aldrich "has evidently taken a fancy to the Hoosier state."

42. The only other professional artist of significance in South Bend in this period was landscape painter Alexis Fournier, who also relocated to the city in 1922.

43. The Oliver Hotel show was practically a solo for Aldrich, for it presented fifty-four of his paintings, plus six by Chicago artist George Hamilton Thomas. "Art-Loving Public of South Bend Given Rare Opportunity in Exhibit," *South Bend News-Times*, January 26, 1922, scr 36/A23, and South Bend Public Library local history files.

44. Eugenie married writer and cartoonist J. P. McEvoy in February 1923; they were divorced in 1932. She later married musician Phillip Odell. Continuing her career as a painter, Eugenie was associated with the Woodstock Artists Association and exhibited with the Salons of America and elsewhere. Information about Esta Grantham is taken from the notice of her marriage to Aldrich on December 24, 1922, in "Bride of Today," scr 46/A48.

45. Accounts of the founding of the Fine Arts Club are given in "Organization for Study of Art Plan of Local Artists," scr 35/A18, "Organization of Artists Formed," scr 34/A16, and untitled clippings, scr 62/A54, 62/A56. Aldrich's pupils in South Bend included Harold Arthur Roney, who made his career in Texas. An example of Aldrich's newspaper columns, "South Bend Art Circles," dating to about 1930, is in his scrapbook (35/A21).

46. "Studio Notes," *Art News* 22 (July 19, 1924): 4.

47. The year 1924 was one of Aldrich's most professionally active. Michael David Zellman, *300 Years of American Art* (Secaucus, NJ: Wellfleet Press, 1987), 1:649, states that he received a traveling scholarship that year that took him to the American Academy in Rome; the information is repeated in Falk, *Who Was Who in American Art 1574–1965*, 1:77, but corroborated nowhere else and is probably erroneous. Aldrich is highly unlikely either to have received such an award as a fifty-three-year-old professional artist or to have neglected to add it to his inflated credentials.

48. On Aldrich's participation in the Davenport group exhibition: "Exhibit of Fine Paintings Will Be Held Here," *Davenport Democrat and Leader*, April 14, 1926, and "Pictures by G. Ames Aldrich Exhibited Here," *Davenport Democrat and Leader*, April 23, 1926. On the Rockford and Fort Wayne exhibitions: "Local Artists Honored," *South Bend Tribune*, March 25, 1926 (scr 29/A6). On his 1926 visit to Rock Island: "Noted Artist and His Family Guets [*sic*] of Mr. and Mrs. Swan at New Fort Armstrong Hotel" and "G. Ames Aldrich, Famous Artist, to Be in Rock Island," scr 31/A10.

49. R. A. Lennon, "Paintings by Gross, Grigware and Aldrich," *Chicago Evening Post Magazine of the Art World*, January 18, 1927. The three-man exhibition was also written up in the club's journal ("Painters and Sculptors Honor Art Benefactors," *Palette and Chisel* 4 [January 1927]: 2). Aldrich's prizes included the Municipal Art League's Thompson prize for an Illinois landscape in the Art Institute's 1926 *Chicago and Vicinity* exhibition and purchase prizes at the Chicago Galleries Association exhibitions twice in 1926 and in 1928 and 1929.

50. The painting exhibited in the Sesquicentennial Exposition was *Frankenstein*, winner of the Thompson prize in the 1926 *Chicago and Vicinity* exhibition. *Christmas Eve, Montreuil-sur-Mer* was submitted for the 1926 Carnegie International exhibition but rejected by the jury (*Record of the Carnegie Institute's International Exhibitions 1896–1996* [Madison, CT: Sound View Press, 1998], 13).

51. Aldrich won the Indiana University Alumni Association prize for a winter scene in 1926, the Downs prize for an industrial scene along the Illinois Central Railroad in 1929, and the Banks winter landscape prize in 1932.

52. In 1926 Aldrich was living in Aurora, according to his listing in the catalogue of the Chicago Galleries Association annual members' exhibition of that year. The Aldriches occupied a succession of addresses in the Hyde Park and Kenwood neighborhoods on Chicago's South Side. In late 1926, the Chicago telephone directory listed him at 1308 E. 56th Street. In 1928, the Commission for the Encouragement of Local Art sent a letter to Aldrich at 1026 E. 46th Street (information from Joel Dryer), where the family was recorded as still living in 1930, according to census records. His address in the 1931 edition of *American Art Directory* was 1102 E. 46th Street, which is confirmed by the telephone directory (his first listing since 1926). He remained listed there through 1938, but around that time he apparently moved to 5647 S. Blackstone, according to Marcia Morrison, whose aunt and uncle lived in the same six-flat apartment building (Marcia Morrison to Peter Lundberg, February 6, 2006, Lundberg Aldrich files). In telephone directories for June 1940 and March 1941 and in his obituary in the *Chicago Tribune* on March 8, 1941, his address is 5521 S. Kimbark.

53. No details of his 1929 European trip survive. Aldrich returned alone from Liverpool in October, according to a ship manifest. He is said to have been a frequent summer visitor to Jackson, Michigan, and many locals acquired his paintings (information kindly supplied by Tessa Eger, Jackson District Library, Jackson, Michigan). The family's trip to Rochester is noted as the second in two years (Aldrich having first visited there around 1918) in

"Painters 'Keep Up with the Times,' George Ames Aldrich, Here, Avers," *Rochester Post,* July 18, 1931, scr 45/A46.

54. Aldrich's column "South Bend Art Circles" (scr 35/A21) can be dated to about 1930 as it mentions the artist's daughter, Betty, born in 1924, as a six-year-old.

55. "Found Summer Colony at Lake Wawasee," *Chicago Evening Post,* August 2, 1932, and unidentified clipping, scr 37/A28. Nashville, Indiana, the center of the Brown County artists' colony, was also listed as Aldrich's summer home, in Mrs. H. B. Burnet, *Art Guide to Indiana* (Bloomington: Extension Division, Indiana University, 1931), 141, but this is not noted elsewhere, nor have any paintings of Brown County scenery been attributed to him.

56. Untitled article, *Christian Science Monitor,* January 15, 1932. This appears to be the same painting illustrated in the *American Magazine of Art* 15 (September 1924): 491, and in an untitled clipping, probably dating to 1924, scr 40/A38.

57. Information from Peter Lundberg, based on interviews with South Bend–area residents who had known Aldrich or whose relatives had shared their memories.

58. Information from Dave Makielski, grandson of Joseph and Theodora Makielski, Edwardsburg, Michigan, and from Bradley Vite, Bradley Vite Fine Arts, Elkhart, Indiana. An undated article in the Elgin State Hospital newsletter described him as "an old friend" whose name had been mentioned "many times" (scr 47/A49). This and a note about the artist in another hospital newsletter (scr 47/A50), in which he is quoted as having specialized in the painting of running water "for forty years," appear to be from the last two years of his life.

59. Esta is listed as a teacher at Chicago's Tilden High School in the 1930 census; data was taken in April, making it likely that she had returned to work at the September start of the school year and thus before the stock market crash in October 1929. In 1934 Aldrich was dropped from membership in the Arts Club of Chicago for failure to pay dues (membership records, Arts Club of Chicago Papers, series 6, box 8, Newberry Library, Chicago); this was not necessarily a result of straitened finances, but in Aldrich's case that seems likely. On at least one occasion, friends came to Aldrich's aid by buying paintings (Marcia Morrison to Peter Lundberg, February 6, 2006, Lundberg Aldrich files).

60. In the 1930s he also dropped his prices and placed paintings with several dealers. On reproductions of Aldrich's paintings in the 1930s, see the following essay in this volume.

61. The exception was a show in his home in 1936 (C. J. Bulliet, "Around the Galleries: Studio Exhibition," *Chicago Daily News,* December 5, 1936; printed announcement, scr 55/31).

62. Estimate courtesy of Peter Lundberg. Obituaries appeared in the *New York Times* and the *Chicago Tribune* (both on March 8, 1941), as well as in several regional newspapers (scr 48/A51–53).

FROM MONTREUIL TO THE MIDWEST: ALDRICH'S ART IN CONTEXT

The opening quotation is from R. A. Lennon, "Paintings by Gross, Grigware and Aldrich," *Chicago Evening Post,* January 18, 1927.

Items from Aldrich's scrapbook of clippings and other ephemera in the collection of Peter Lundberg (hereafter "scr") are cited here by page/item numbers assigned by Mr. Lundberg. For many of the newspaper clippings in the scrapbook, sources and publication dates are unknown.

1. "Painters and Sculptors Honor Art Benefactors," *Palette & Chisel* 4 (January 1927): 2.

2. *Winter, The Brandywine* was the title of one of Aldrich's paintings shown in the inaugural Hoosier Salon exhibition of 1925.

3. Estimate courtesy of Peter Lundberg.

4. On Aldrich painting portraits in the South Bend area, see scr 38/A33 and "Plan Art Exhibit," 34/A13; on his work in still life, "Woman's Club Hears Art Critic from Illinois," scr 40/A37; on his "modernistic pictures": "Ball State Opens New Exhibit Sunday," scr 39/A36; on painting in Alabama: "Painters 'Keep Up with the Times,' George Ames Aldrich, Here, Avers," *Rochester Post,* July 18, 1931, scr 45/A46.

5. On the newly subordinate role of pictures in home decorating after the turn of the century, see William S. Ayres, "Pictures in the American Home, 1880–1930," in *The Arts and the American Home, 1890–1930,* ed. Jessica H. Foy and Karal Ann Marling (Knoxville: University of Tennessee Press, 1994), 149–164; on the aesthetic principles constituting "good taste" in the early twentieth century, see Bradley C. Brooks, "Clarity, Contrast, and Simplicity: Changes in American Interiors, 1880–1930," in the same volume, especially p. 28. "Pictures Now Bought to Suit Decorations," *Chicago Evening Post Magazine of the Art World,* March 1, 1927; see also Lena M. McCauley, "Pictures Valued in Interior Decoration," *Chicago Evening Post News of the Art World,* December 11, 1917, and C.H.B. [Charles H. Burkholder], "Pictures in the Home," *Bulletin of the Art Institute of Chicago* 14 (March 1920): 34. Of the art that represented "excellent decorative value," the authors of one popular decorating book singled out "landscape-and-architecture subjects" as offering "excellent decorative value" (Harold Donaldson Eberlein, Abbot McClure, and Edward Stratton Holloway, *The Practical Book of Interior Decoration* [Philadelphia: J. B. Lippincott Company, 1919], 350, 352).

6. On Tonalism, see David A. Cleveland, *A History of American Tonalism: 1880–1920* (Manchester and New York: Hudson Hills Press, 2010).

7. In the 1923 edition of the *American Art Directory,* Aldrich listed the Tree Studios building as his studio address but Montreuil-sur-Mer as his "home." The names Montreuil and Montreuil-sur-Mer are commonly used interchangeably.

8. Brooks, "Clarity, Contrast, and Simplicity," 22, 34–37. See also Karen Halttunen, "From Parlor to Living Room: Domestic Space, Interior Decoration and the Culture of Personality," in *Consuming Visions: Accumulation and Display of Goods in America, 1880–1920,* ed. Simon J. Bronner (New York: W. W. Norton & Company, 1989), 182–184.

9. William H. Truettner and Roger B. Stein, eds., *Picturing Old New England: Image and Memory* (Washington, DC: Smithsonian American Art Museum, 1999), 103–104, 164–166.

10. Aldrich and Holslag shared a studio in Chicago's Tree Studios building and both were members of the Palette and Chisel Club, of which Holslag served as president. According to "Aldrich Exhibit Is Praised by Aurora Artist," scr 38/A32, they painted together in Gloucester. Holslag's *Gloucester Harbor* is dated 1919, the first year Aldrich painted in the New England fishing port. His own *Gloucester Docks* likely dates to the same time. Citing Holslag's *Gloucester Harbor,* a reviewer contrasted Holslag's vigorous manner to Aldrich's soft, "melancholy" style (Frederic Paul Hull Thompson, "Twenty-third Annual Exhibition of Chicago Artists," *Fine Arts Journal* 37 [March 1919]: 12).

11. G. Ames Aldrich, "South Bend Art Circles," scr 35/A21.

12. A Gary newspaper assumed that *Steel,* exhibited in that city in a traveling version of the 1929 Hoosier Salon exhibition, was an interpretation of Gary's mills ("Painting of Gary Mills to Be Hung at Hoosier Salon," Lundberg Aldrich files). In 1932, the same work or a related, identically titled one was listed in the catalogue of Aldrich's solo exhibition at Ball State Teachers College in Muncie as having been painted in South Chicago. Another interpretation of this theme was a painting titled *Industry,* which according to one description pictured the steel mill in full operation at twilight (unidentified newspaper clipping, scr 63/A60).

13. "River Forest Women's Club," *Oak Parker,* February 26, 1926; see also Arietta Wimer Towne, "Art Notes," *Oak Leaves,* January 21, 1927.

14. Lennon, "Paintings by Gross, Grigware and Aldrich."

15. Judith Vale Newton and Carol Weiss, *A Grand Tradition: The Art and Artists of the Hoosier Salon, 1925–1990* (Indianapolis: Hoosier Salon Patrons Association, 1993), 2, 152. *Frankenstein* was awarded the Municipal Art League's Thompson prize for an Illinois landscape painting in the 1926 *Chicago and Vicinity* exhibition.

16. Lennon, "Paintings by Gross, Grigware and Aldrich."

17. On the facts and fictions of Aldrich's early years, see the biographical essay.

18. "Art Society Buys Famous Painting," *Sioux City Daily Tribune,* July 8, 1919 (Lundberg Aldrich files).

19. In the Sesquicentennial Exposition, Aldrich was represented by *Frankenstein.*

20. Thaulow's *Nocturne* was reproduced in *International Studio* in 1897 and in *Brush and Pencil* in 1903; his Washerwomen at Quimperlé (or Washing at Quimperlé) was reproduced in the same *Brush and Pencil* article and was the subject of reproductive prints by Thaulow and others. Aldrich dated two versions of *Washerwomen at Quimperlé* to 1921, following his return from his second trip to France in January of that year.

21. Gabriel P. Weisberg et al., *Collecting in the Gilded Age: Art Patronage in Pittsburgh, 1890–1910* (Pittsburgh: Frick Art & Historical Center, 1997), 24.

22. On Aldrich's claim to have been Thaulow's "private pupil": *Sioux City Daily Tribune,* July 8, 1919; his "favorite pupil": "Paintings to Be Exhibited Today at C. of C.," scr 46/A47; his "painting companion": "The Art of G. Ames Aldrich," undated brochure, in Lundberg Aldrich files, and "Art Exhibit Opens Today at Ball State College," scr 39/A35.

23. See the biographical essay in this volume.

24. Evelyn Marie Stuart, "Public Palaces and Their Art Treasures," *Fine Arts Journal* 35 (October 1917): 47.

25. Thompson, "Twenty-third Annual Exhibition of Chicago Artists," 12.

26. Weisberg et al., *Collecting in the Gilded Age,* 241–246; Candace J. Adelson, "Fritz Thaulow's *The Stream:* George Eastman and Impressionism," *Porticus: Journal of the Memorial Art Gallery of the University of Rochester* 17–19 (1994–96): 45–49. I am grateful to Vidar Poulsson for bringing Adelson's article to my attention.

27. Darcy Lewis, "Reconsidering a Familiar Work: Thaulow's *Thawing Ice," Wright Angles* 3 (November-December 2004/January 2005): 3–4.

28. Edward G. Holden, "In the Field of Art," *Chicago Tribune,* January 18, 1903.

29. These, along with another accessioned in 1939, were removed from the collection in the late 1940s. Ironically, in 2004 the Art Institute acquired yet another Thaulow: one of several versions of the pastel *Melting Snow* (2004.86). See Lewis, "Reconsidering a Familiar Work."

30. Edward Howard Moore, "Fritz Thaulow, Norway's Master of Color," *Brush and Pencil* 13 (October 1903): 1–5.

31. Gabriel Mourey, "Fritz Thaulow – The Man and the Artist," *International Studio* 2 (July 1897): 3.

32. "Public Approves Exhibit of Work by Chicagoans," *Chicago Tribune,* February 11, 1917.

33. "The Home Forum," *Christian Science Monitor,* January 15, 1932; "South Bend Woman's Club," scr 39/A34.

34. On the central role of women's organizations in the art movement of the Progressive Era see Karen Blair, *The Torchbearers: Women and Their Amateur Arts Associations in America, 1890–1930* (Bloomington: Indiana University Press, 1994), chapter 4. On the tendency toward exhibitions of uncontroversial art, especially landscape, see p. 86.

35. "Local Owners of Painters' Works," *Rock Island Union,* January 10, 1917. On the Art Institute's involvement in the promotion of art in the hinterland, see for example "Notes. Department of Extension," *Bulletin of the Art Institute of Chicago* 10 (December 1916): 240, and "The Growth of Extension Work," *Bulletin of the Art Institute of Chicago* 14 (March 1920): 50, 53–54.

36. "Artist Shows World's Beauty," scr 37/A27; "Painters 'Keep Up with the Times,' George Ames Aldrich, Here, Avers"; "Noted Artist and His Family Guets [*sic*] of Mr. and Mrs. Swan at New Fort Armstrong Hotel," scr 33/A12.

37. "Art Society Buys Famous Painting," *Sioux City Daily Tribune,* July 8, 1919 (Lundberg Aldrich files); "Eminent Artist to Exhibit Here," scr 34/A15.

38. "G. Ames Aldrich, Famous Artist, to Be in Rock Island," scr 31/A10; "Noted Artist and His Family Guets [*sic*] of Mr. and Mrs. Swan at New Fort Armstrong Hotel."

39. "Eminent Artist to Exhibit Here," scr 34/A15; "Painters 'Keep Up with the Times,' George Ames Aldrich, Here, Avers."

40. Advertisement for Young's Art Galleries, *Chicago Tribune,* March 5, 1916. In Chicago Aldrich's work was also handled by the Newcomb-Macklin frame company; his commercial venues outside Chicago included the Makielski art shop in Edwardsburg, Michigan; Grable's Art and Gift Shop in Oak Park, Illinois; and the Ruth E. Patten decorative arts shop in Kokomo, Indiana.

41. "Well Known Artist to Exhibit at Stockwell," *Lafayette Journal and Courier,* scr 36/A24; "Bride of Today," scr 46/A48.

42. Chicago dealer J. W. Young recalled Aldrich as "a well-bred, gentlemanly sort of chap" (J. W. Young to Nettie McKinnon, April 29, 1944, Nettie J. McKinnon Art Collection files, La Grange Elementary District 102, La Grange, IL).

43. "Art Society Buys Famous Painting."

44. Information from Peter Lundberg, based on interviews with South Bend–area residents who had known Aldrich or whose relatives had shared their memories.

45. "Interesting Exhibit at Lieber's," scr 45/A45; the article notes that Aldrich "has evidently taken a fancy to the Hoosier state. . . ." The Oliver Hotel show presented fifty-four Aldrich paintings plus six by Chicago artist George Hamilton Thomas. "Art-Loving Public of South Bend Given Rare Opportunity in Exhibit," scr 36/A23.

46. "The Art of G. Ames Aldrich." Aldrich is listed in the South Bend directory as living at the Mar-Main in 1925 only. Given his ever-precarious finances, it is possible that he painted the murals in both the Mar-Main and the Oliver Hotel in exchange for rent.

47. On the Fine Arts Club, see "Organization of Artists Formed," scr 34/A16; "Organization for Study of Art Plan of Local Artists," scr 35/A18; and clipping fragments, scr 62/A54, 62/A56, 62/A57. The club was still in existence around 1930, when Aldrich mentioned it in "South Bend Art Circles," scr 35/A21; this source can be dated to around 1930 as it notes his daughter, born in 1924, as a six-year-old.

48. "Aldrich to Paint at Club Exhibit," scr 37/A30; "Plan Stag Night for Art Exhibit," scr 37/A29.

49. "Woman's Club Hears Art Critic from Illinois," scr 40/A37.

50. Sponsored by fifty clubs, mostly women's clubs, the Hoosier Salon was another manifestation of the influence of such organizations on art life, and on art taste as well, during the Progressive Era.

51. "South Bend Art Circles," scr 35/A21. On the dating of this article, see note 46.

52. "Found Summer Colony at Lake Wawasee," *Chicago Evening Post,* August 2, 1932.

53. Information courtesy of Peter Lundberg, Dave Makielski, and Bradley Vite.

54. His connection to Aurora probably came about through his former studio-mate Holslag, who had lived there and who remained involved in its art

life. Holslag's visit to Aldrich's Aurora exhibition in 1924 is recorded in "Aldrich Exhibit is Praised by Aurora Artist," scr 38/A32, which describes the two as longtime painting companions.

55. Information on R. H. Conklin supplied by Mike Ficheel, Aurora Historical Society.

56. Conklin was almost certainly responsible for the undated brochure "The Art of G. Ames Aldrich."

57. "Society. Exhibition of Paintings," *Aurora Beacon-News,* April 30, 1924, scr 32/A28; brief notices in *Art News* 22 (May 17, 1924): 4, and *Art News* 22 (July 19, 1924): 8; "Many Aldrich Paintings Will Remain in City," scr 42/A42.

58. "Woman's Club Hears Art Critic from Illinois," scr 40/A37; R. H. Conklin, "Homes in Middle West Being Made Beautiful," *Chicago Evening Post,* August 19, 1924, scr 43/A43; "Aldrich Is Unexcelled, Declare Noted Critics Here for His Exhibit," scr 41/A41.

59. "Art Not Merely Women's Pastime and Artists Not Freaks – Aldrich," scr 41/A39.

60. "Aldrich to Paint at Club Exhibit," scr 37/A30; "Art Not Merely Women's Pastime and Artists Not Freaks – Aldrich"; "Art Foundation of Business, Artist's Belief," scr 29/A3; "George Ames Aldrich, Well Known Painter, Spending Week-end Here," scr 34/A14.

61. Email from Martha Hopkins Dean to Peter Lundberg, December 15, 1998, regarding her grandfather Arthur Hopkins, in Lundberg Aldrich files.

62. Information on Cowan's collecting and public display of Aldrich paintings from email correspondence, Jim Womack to Peter Lundberg, January 24, 2010, Lundberg Aldrich files; "Winter – The Brandywine," scr 40/A38; Lincoln J. Carter, Jr., "Fine Paintings by G. Ames Aldrich in Middle West Homes," scr 36/A22. Not surprisingly, the only "foreign" canvas in Cowan's collection was a Thaulow painting, *Old Mill Stream* ("Large Crowd at Art Institute," *Decatur Review,* December 1, 1924).

63. Roy C. Haines, "Voice of the People. On Art Exhibit," *Aurora Beacon-News,* April 30, 1924, scr 32/A48.

64. Carter, "Fine Paintings by G. Ames Aldrich in Middle West Homes"; "Woman's Club Hears Art Critic from Illinois," scr 40/A37.

65. President of the Southern States Art League, quoted in "The Art of G. Ames Aldrich."

66. Explanatory text on verso of 1938 calendar issued by Caswell's National Crest Coffee (collection of Peter Lundberg).

67. The Hoosier Salon was open to any artist who worked in Indiana, not only to residents. On the Hoosier Salon, see Newton, *A Grand Tradition.* A third venue for self-described conservatives was the Association of Chicago Painters and Sculptors, founded in 1921: Aldrich exhibited with that group in 1927.

68. R. A. Lennon, "Paintings by Gross, Grigware and Aldrich," *Chicago Evening Post,* January 18, 1927; H. I. Brock, "Business Ideas Applied to Art," *Chicago Tribune,* November 1, 1925.

69. "George Ames Aldrich, Well Known Painter, Spending Week-end Here," unidentified Richmond, Indiana, newspaper, May 29, 1932, scr 34/A14.

70. Details of Komar and Melamid's project, launched in 1995, are available at http://awp.diaart.org/km/.

EXHIBITION HISTORY

COMPILED BY WENDY GREENHOUSE

Exact titles of exhibitions are italicized; descriptive titles are romanized.

ABBREVIATIONS

AIC	Art Institute of Chicago, Chicago
CGA	Chicago Galleries Association, Chicago
MF	Marshall Field & Co. galleries, Chicago

1907

April: James Rice Jr.'s gallery, New York

1917

January 12–?: Tri-City Art League, Davenport, Iowa, exhibition of American art organized by the Extension Department, AIC

Elgin Art Association, Elgin, Illinois

1918

February 14–March 17: AIC, *Chicago and Vicinity*

Carson Pirie Scott & Co. Gallery, Chicago, *Works by Chicago Artists*

1919

February 13–March 30: AIC, *Chicago and Vicinity*

1920

January 5–24: Hamilton Club, Chicago, *Chicago Painters of the Forest Preserve of Cook County*

January 29–March 3: AIC, *Chicago and Vicinity*

July: South Shore Country Club, Chicago, *Famous American Painters*

Chicago Society of Artists at the Hamilton Club, Chicago, *Thumbbox Exhibition*

1921

November 3–December 11: AIC, *American Paintings and Sculpture*

1922

January ?–31: Oliver Hotel, South Bend, Indiana, under the auspices of the Civic League, joint exhibition with George H. Thomas

January 26–March 5: AIC, *Chicago and Vicinity*

Carpenter Hotel, Sioux Falls, South Dakota, solo exhibition

Tri-City Art League hall, Davenport, Iowa, solo exhibition [possibly 1921]

1923

April 3–18: Progress Club, South Bend, Indiana, *Fourth Annual Art Exhibition*

May 23–June 2: H. Lieber Company Galleries, Indianapolis, Indiana, solo exhibition

June 20–30: Kokomo Woman's Club at the Carnegie Library, Kokomo, Indiana, solo exhibition

August: Stockwell M. E. Church, Stockwell, Indiana, solo exhibition

1924

May 1–10: Aurora Chamber of Commerce Community Center, Aurora, Illinois, solo exhibition

November 30–December ?: Decatur Art Institute, Decatur, Illinois, exhibition of James M. Cowan collection

December: South Bend Woman's Club, South Bend, Indiana, solo exhibition

1925

January 30–March 10: AIC, *Chicago and Vicinity*

March 9–19: MF, *Hoosier Salon*

April: Newcomb-Macklin Gallery, Chicago, exhibition of modern European and American paintings and prints

1926

January 17–February 7: Richmond Art Association, Richmond, Indiana, annual exhibition

February 4–March 14: AIC, *Chicago and Vicinity*

March 6: The Cameo Salon, Chicago, *Fourth Reception and Program of the Season: Une Soiree Francaise* [*sic*]

March 8–20: MF, *Hoosier Salon*

March 15–April 15: CGA, *Semi-annual Exhibition by the Artist Members*

April 15–24: Blackhawk Hotel, Davenport, Iowa, exhibition of American artists organized by the Aurora Galleries of Fine Arts

April: Fort Wayne, Indiana

April?: Rockford, Illinois

May 29: Ruth E. Patten art shop, Kokomo, Indiana, solo exhibition

May 31–December 1: Sesquicentennial Exposition Department of Fine Arts, Philadelphia, *Exhibition of Paintings, Sculpture and Prints*

September 27–October 16: All-Illinois Society of Fine Arts at Carson, Pirie, Scott and Company galleries, Chicago, *Exhibition by Artists of Illinois*

November 15–December 15: CGA, *Semi-annual Exhibition by the Artist Members*

1927*

January 13–29: CGA, *Paintings by Oskar Gross, Edward Grigware, and George A. Aldrich*

January 31–February 12: MF, *Hoosier Salon*

February 3–March 8: AIC, *Chicago and Vicinity*

May 4–June 1: CGA, *Semi-annual Exhibition by the Artist Members*

October 20–November 12: Association of Chicago Painters and Sculptors at the CGA, *Annual Exhibition*

November 15–December 15: CGA, *Semi-annual Exhibition by the Artist Members*

1928

January 30–February 15: MF, *Hoosier Salon*
February 9–March 21: AIC, *Chicago and Vicinity*
May 1–June 1: CGA, *Semi-annual Exhibition by the Artist Members*
November 15–December 15: CGA, *Semi-annual Exhibition by the Artist Members*
December 14–28: Alden Park Manor, Detroit, solo exhibition

1929*

January 28–February 13: MF, *Hoosier Salon*
December 5–31: CGA, *Semi-annual Exhibition by the Artist Members*

1930

January 27–February 12: MF, *Hoosier Salon*
June 6–12: Hayes Hotel, Jackson, MI, solo exhibition

1931

Alex Johnson Hotel, Rapid City, South Dakota, solo exhibition

1932

January 25–February 6: MF, *Hoosier Salon*
April ?–May 8: Arts Club of Chicago, *Professional Members' Show*
Summer: Spink-Wawasee Hotel, Syracuse, Indiana, solo exhibition
Ball State Teachers Association and Muncie Art Association, Muncie, Indiana, solo exhibition

1933

January 30–February 11: MF, *Hoosier Salon*
May: Ball State Teachers College, Muncie, Indiana, *Exhibition of Paintings by Indiana Artists*

1935

January 28–February 9: MF, *Hoosier Salon*

1936

January 27–February 8: MF, *Hoosier Salon*
November 27–December 16: the artist's home, Chicago, solo exhibition

1937

February 1–13: MF, *Hoosier Salon*

1938

January 31–February 12: MF, *Hoosier Salon*

1939

January 30–February 11: MF, *Hoosier Salon*

YEAR UNKNOWN

March 15–25, circa 1926–1936: Lamar Hotel [Houston?]: joint exhibition with Walter Ufer

* Aldrich may well have participated in the fall 1927 and spring 1929 semi-annual exhibitions by the artist members of the Chicago Galleries Association, for which catalogues are unavailable.

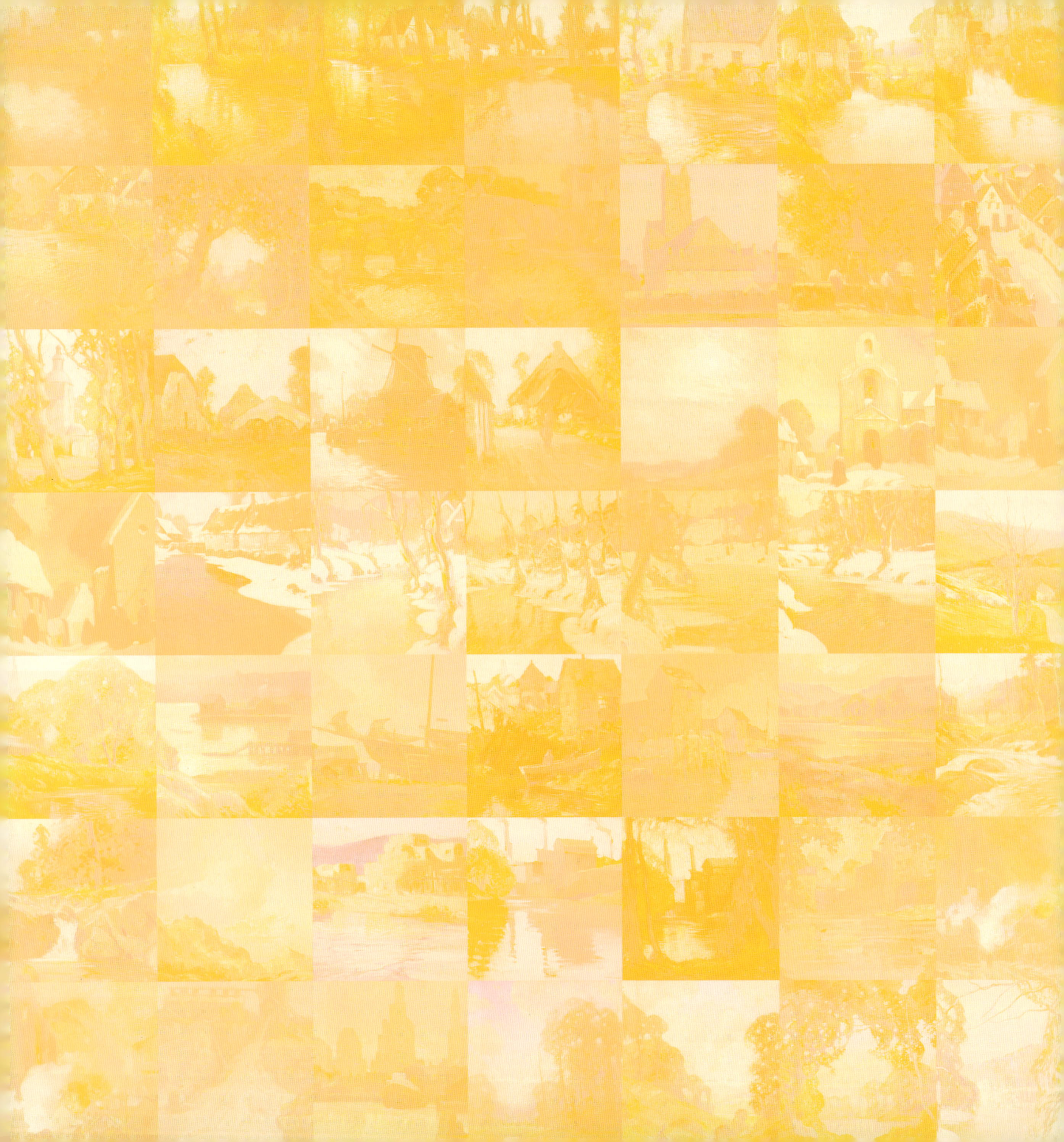

CATALOGUE OF WORKS

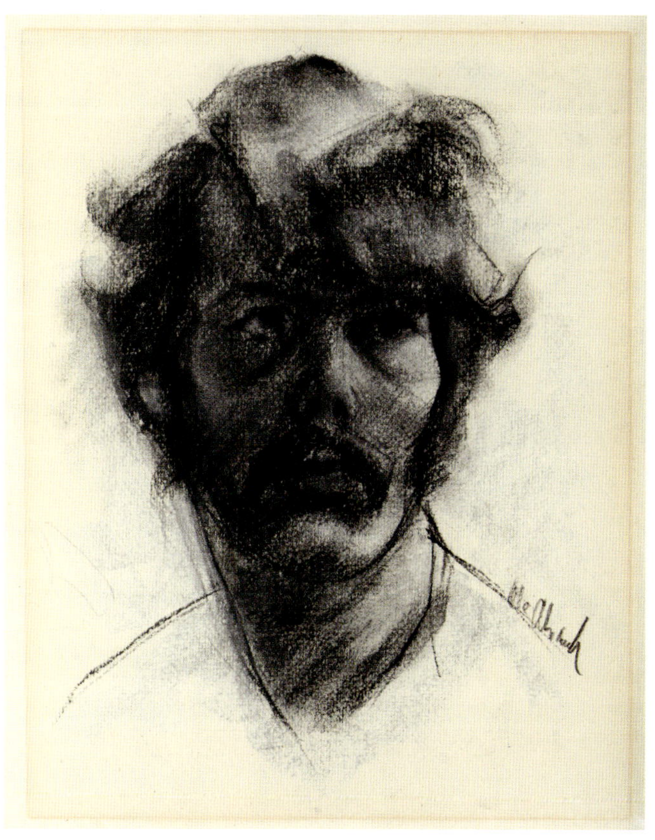

PLATE 1

Me, ca. 1890s

Charcoal on paper, 14 ⅜ × 11 ½ inches

Private Collection

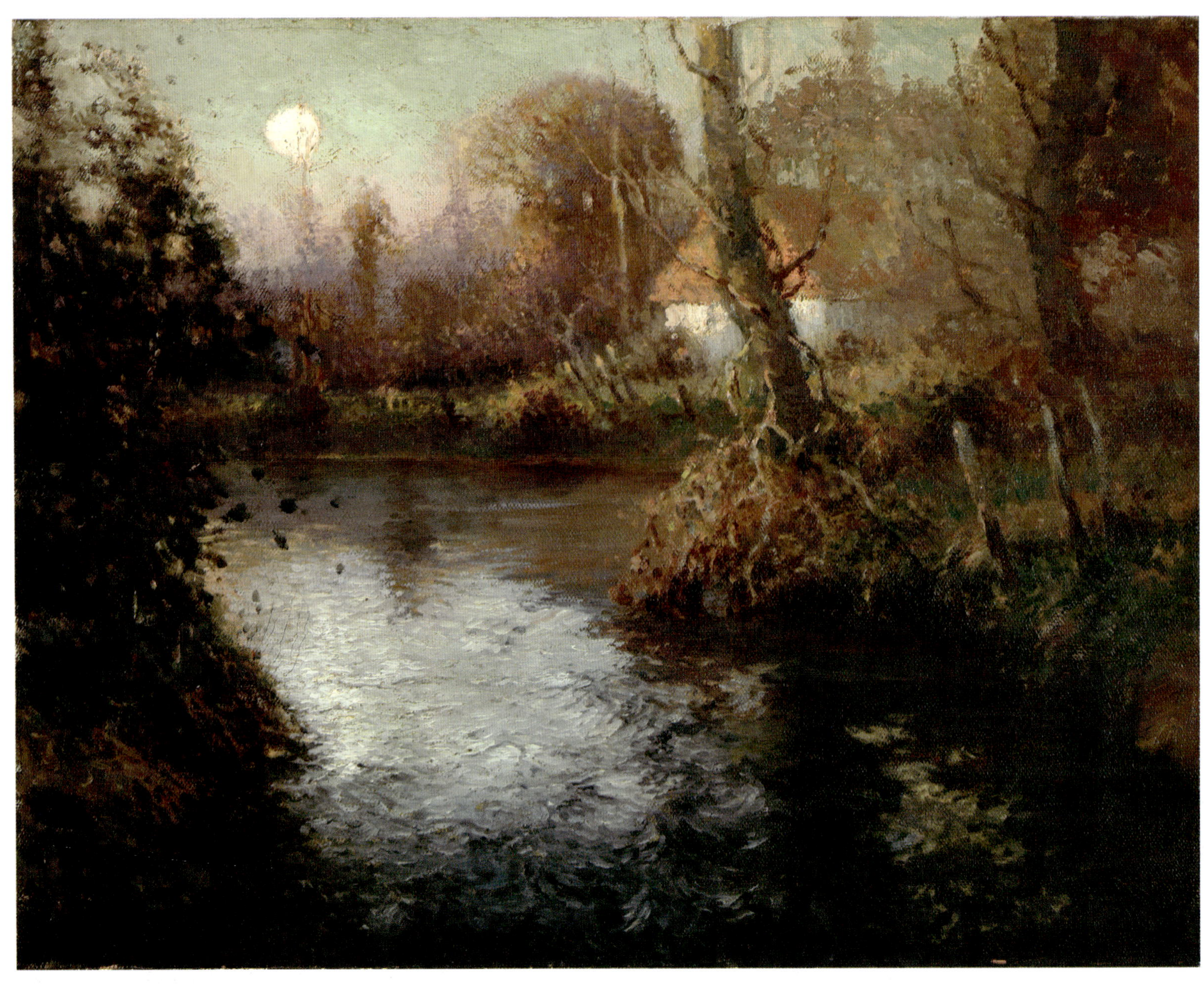

PLATE 2

Le Soir, River Elaune, ca. 1910

Oil on canvas, 16 × 20 inches

Collection of Drs. Nicole and Todd Rozycki

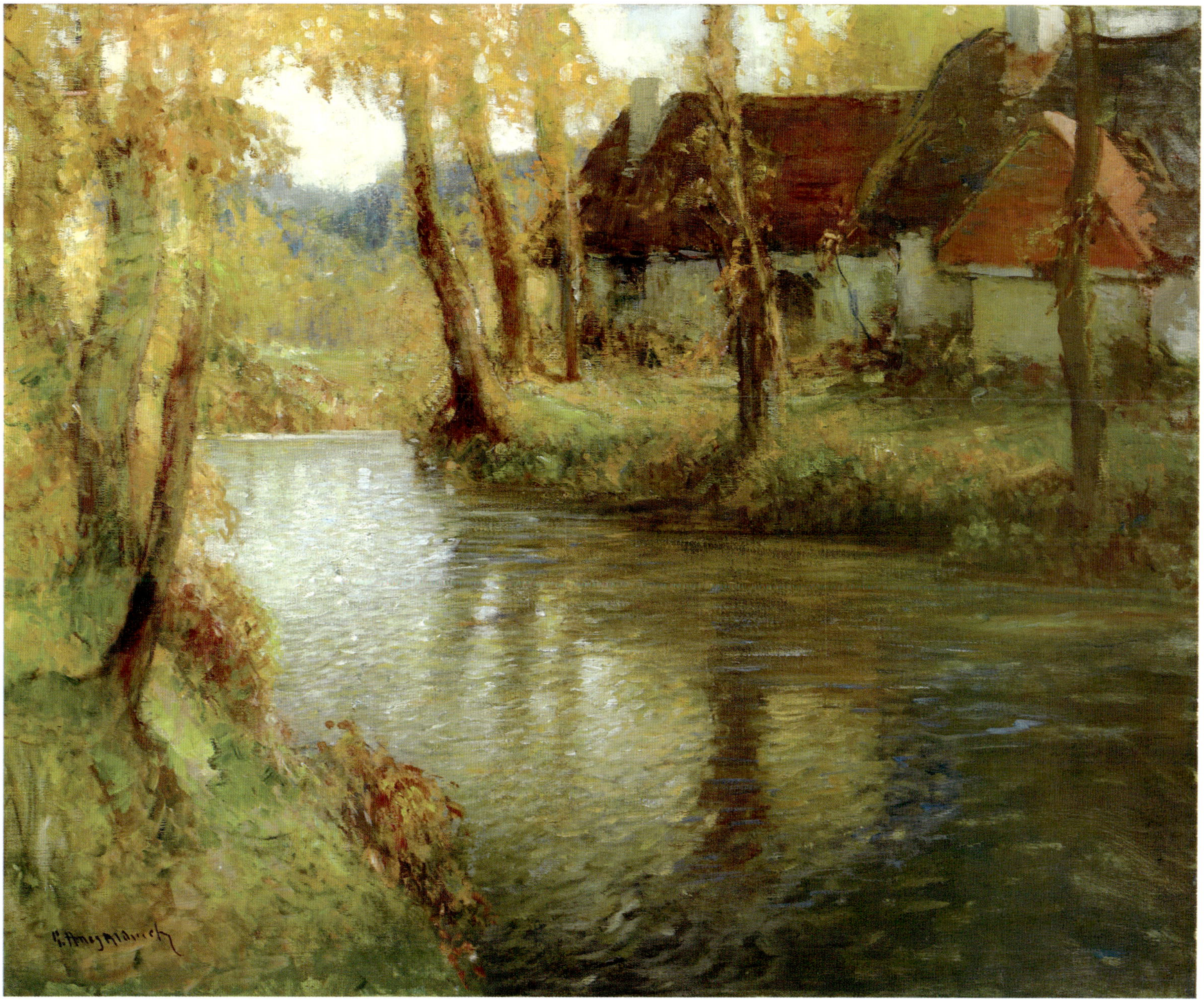

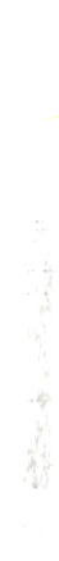

PLATE 3

Untitled (cottages by river, summer), undated

Oil on canvas, 30 × 36 inches

Private Collection

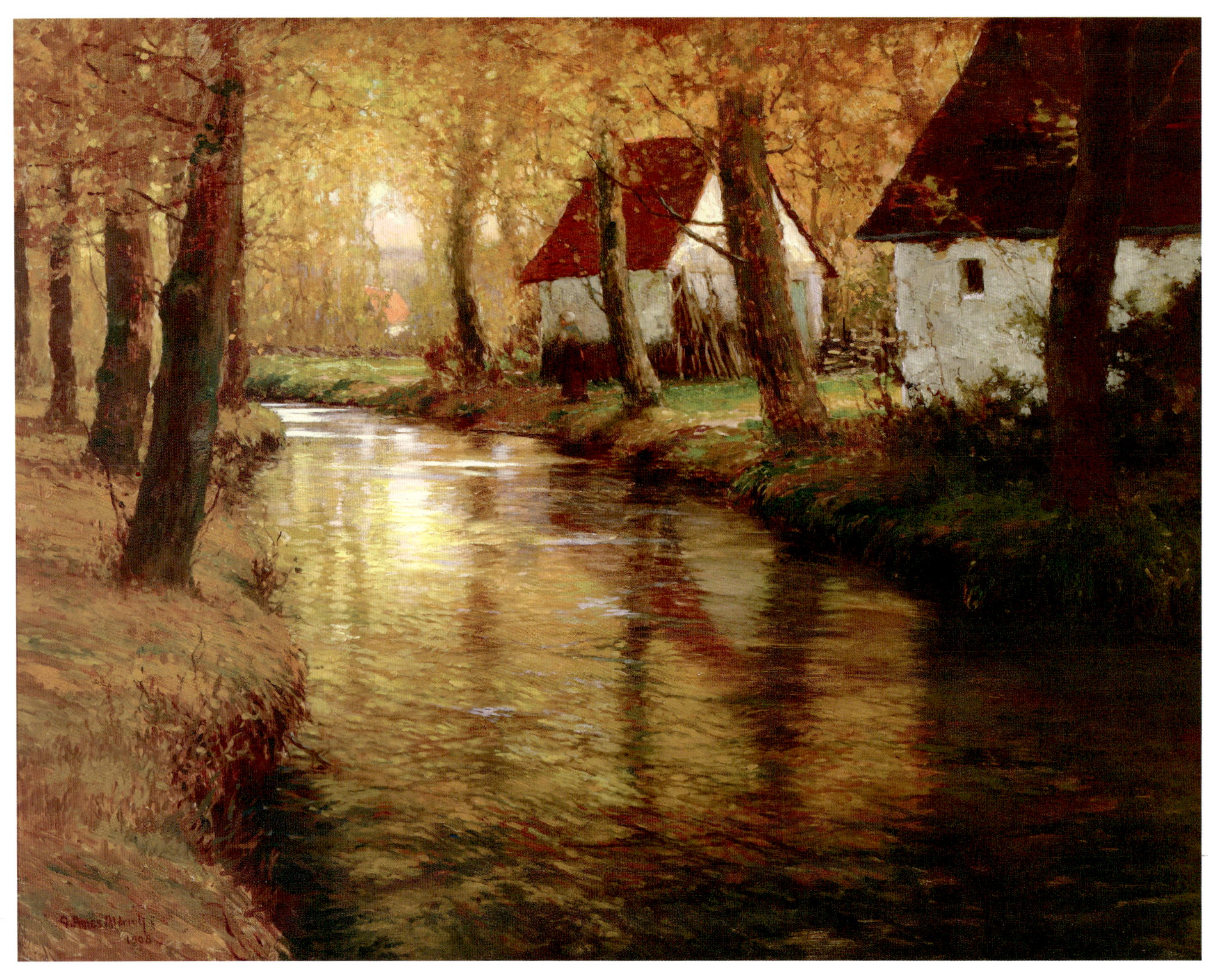

PLATE 4

The River Elaune, Bellengreville, 1908

Oil on canvas, 32 × 40 inches

Brauer Museum of Art, Valparaiso University, 95.08, Gift of Phyllis (Buehner) Duesenberg (VU 1954) and Richard W. Duesenberg (VU 1951, BA, VU 1953, JD)

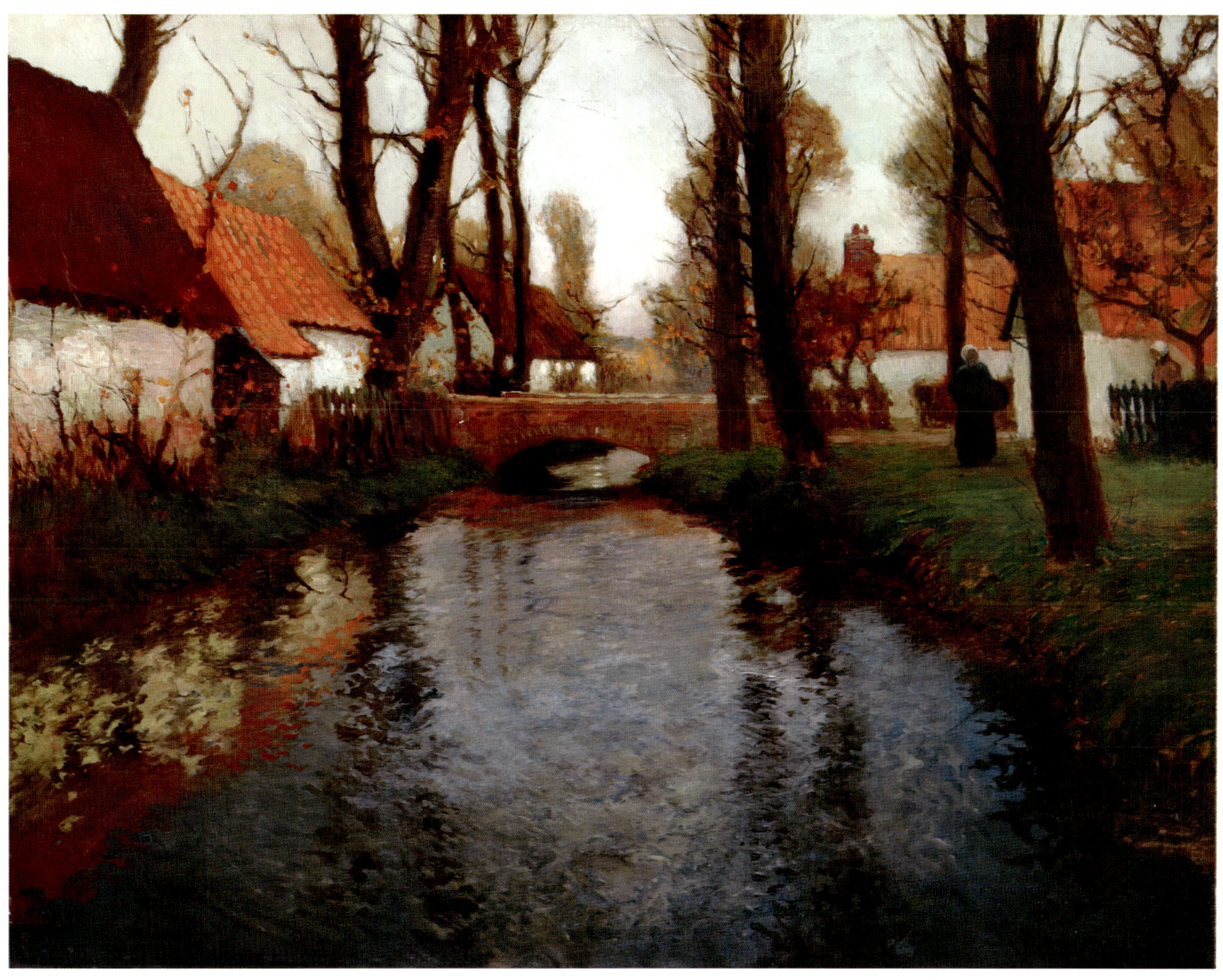

PLATE 5
Old Bridge at Pernois, undated
Oil on canvas, 24 × 30 inches
Collection of Richard and Jean Dennen

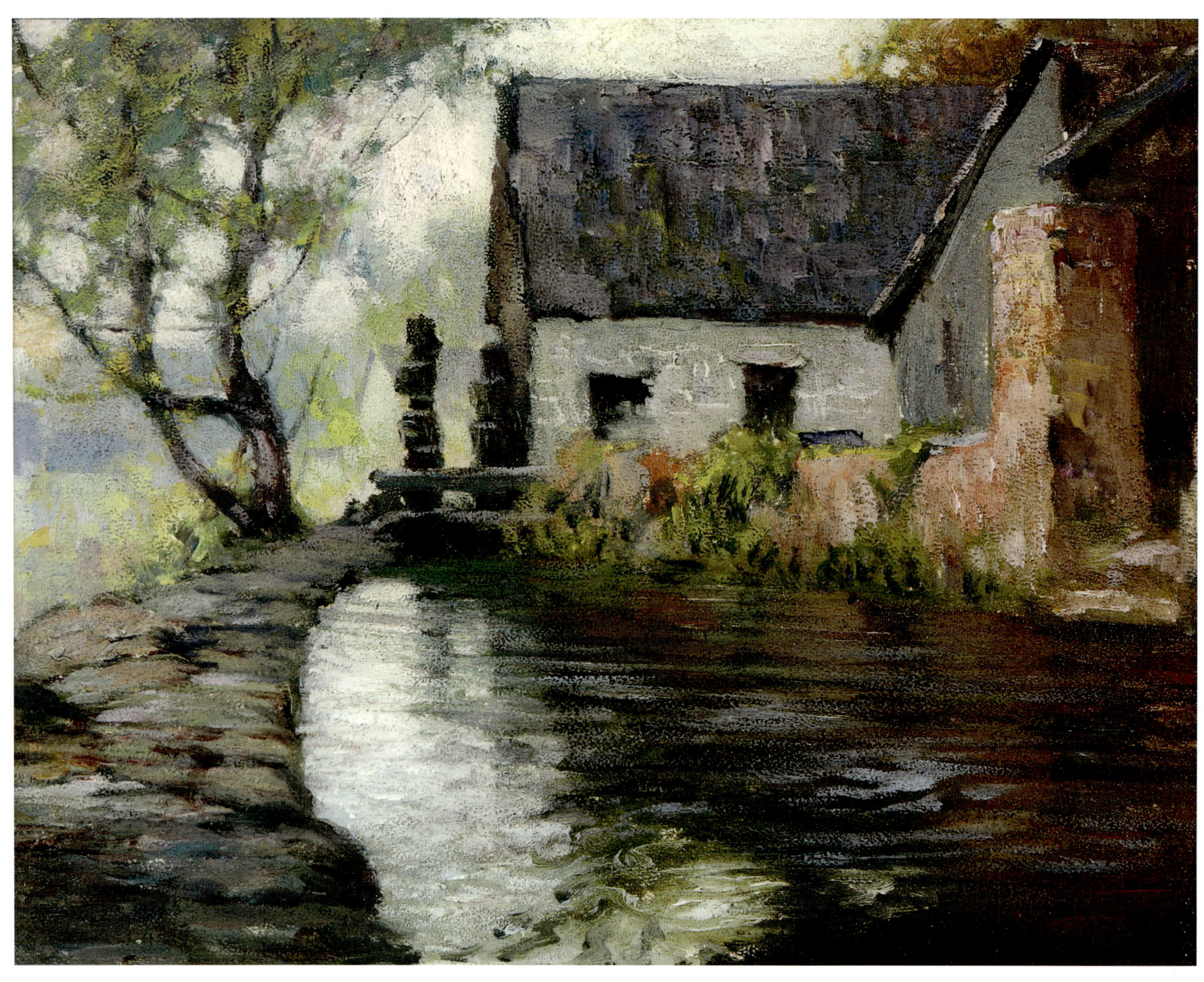

PLATE 6
Pont Aven, Brittany, Finistere, undated
Oil on board, 8 × 10 inches
The Bernie and Sue Konrady Family Collection

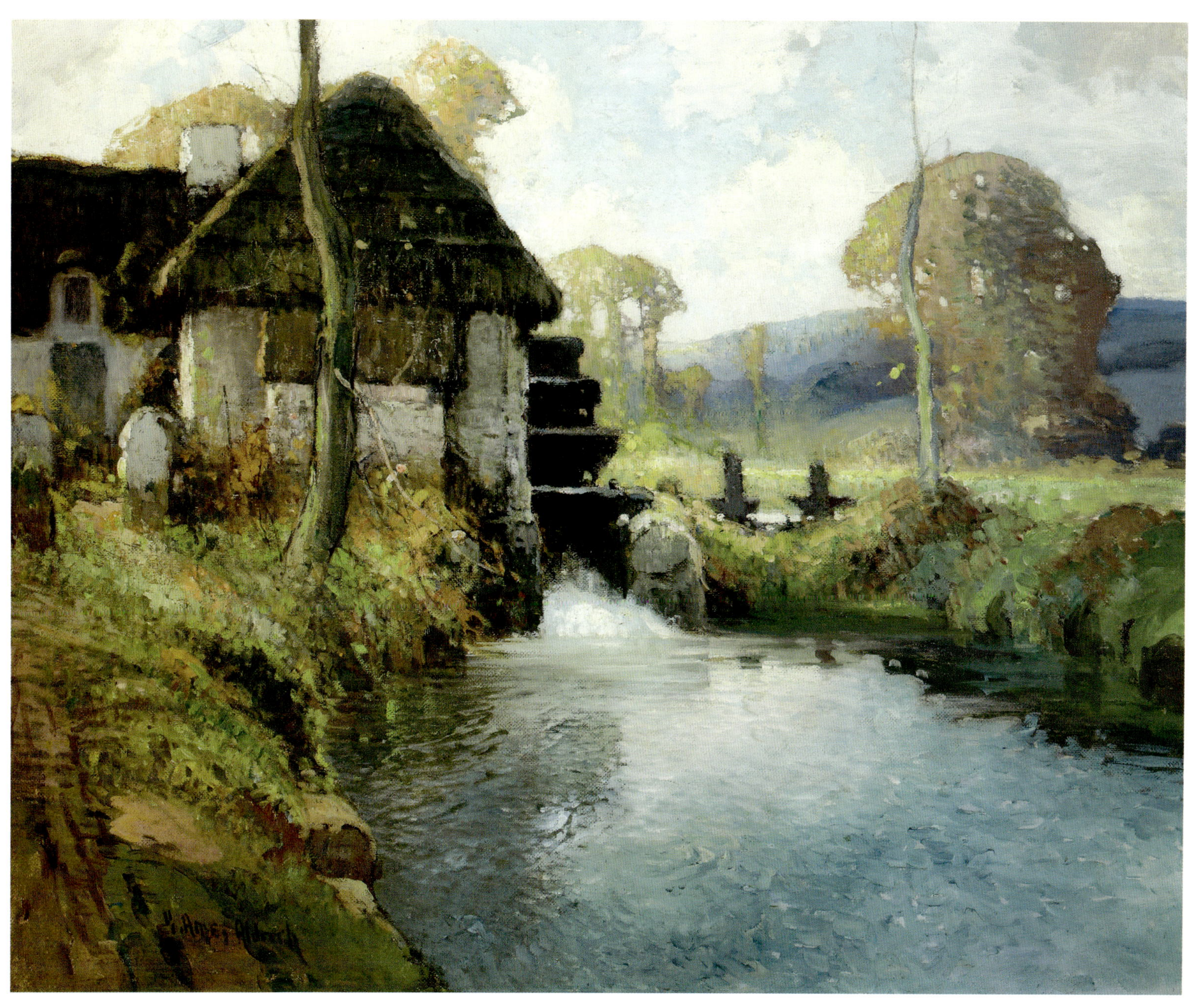

PLATE 7
Brittany Mill, ca. 1925
Oil on board, 30 × 36 inches
Collection of the Charles S. Hayes Family

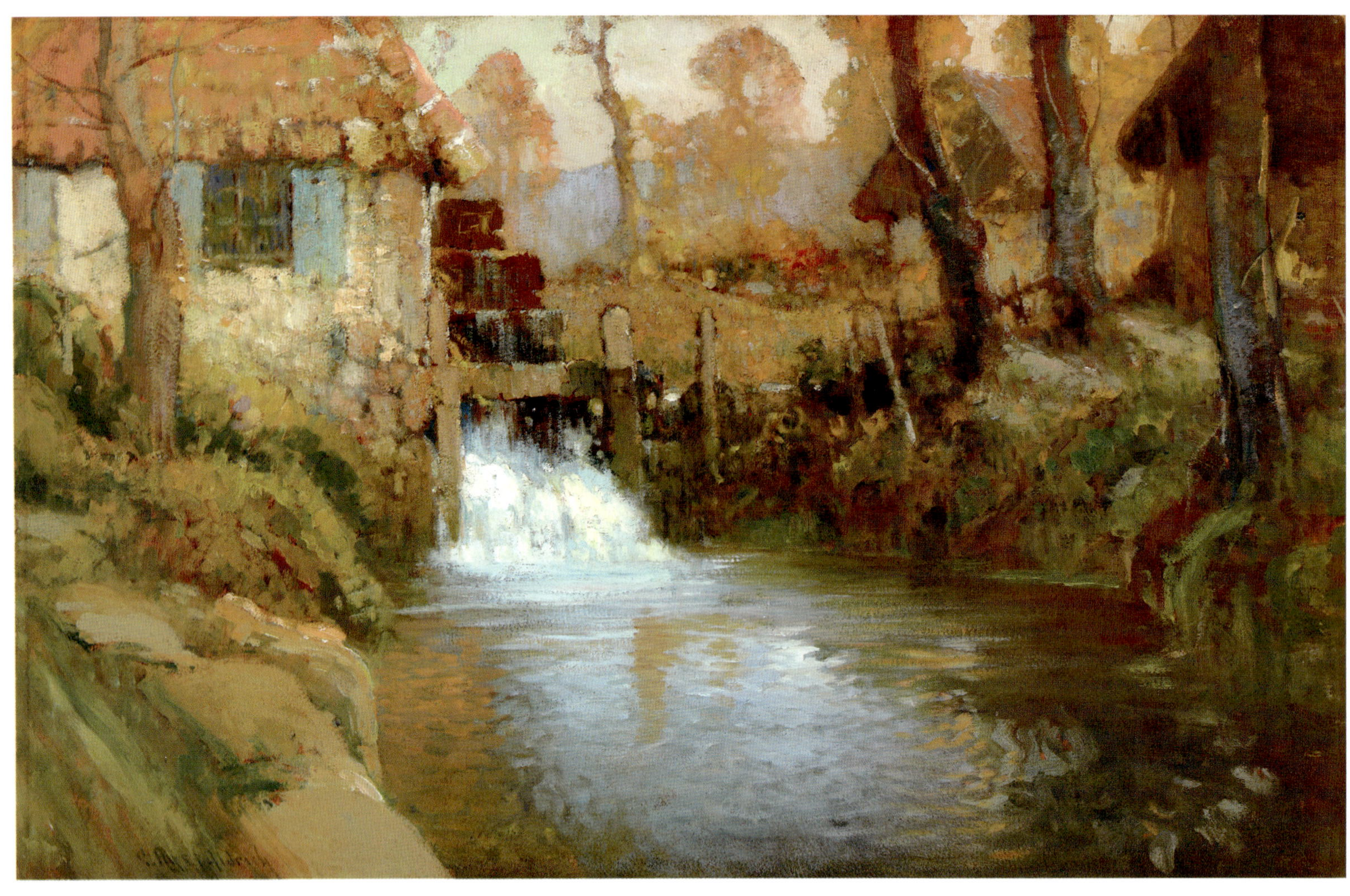

PLATE 8

Untitled (old mill), undated

Oil on board, 23 × 34 inches

Collection of the Charles S. Hayes Family

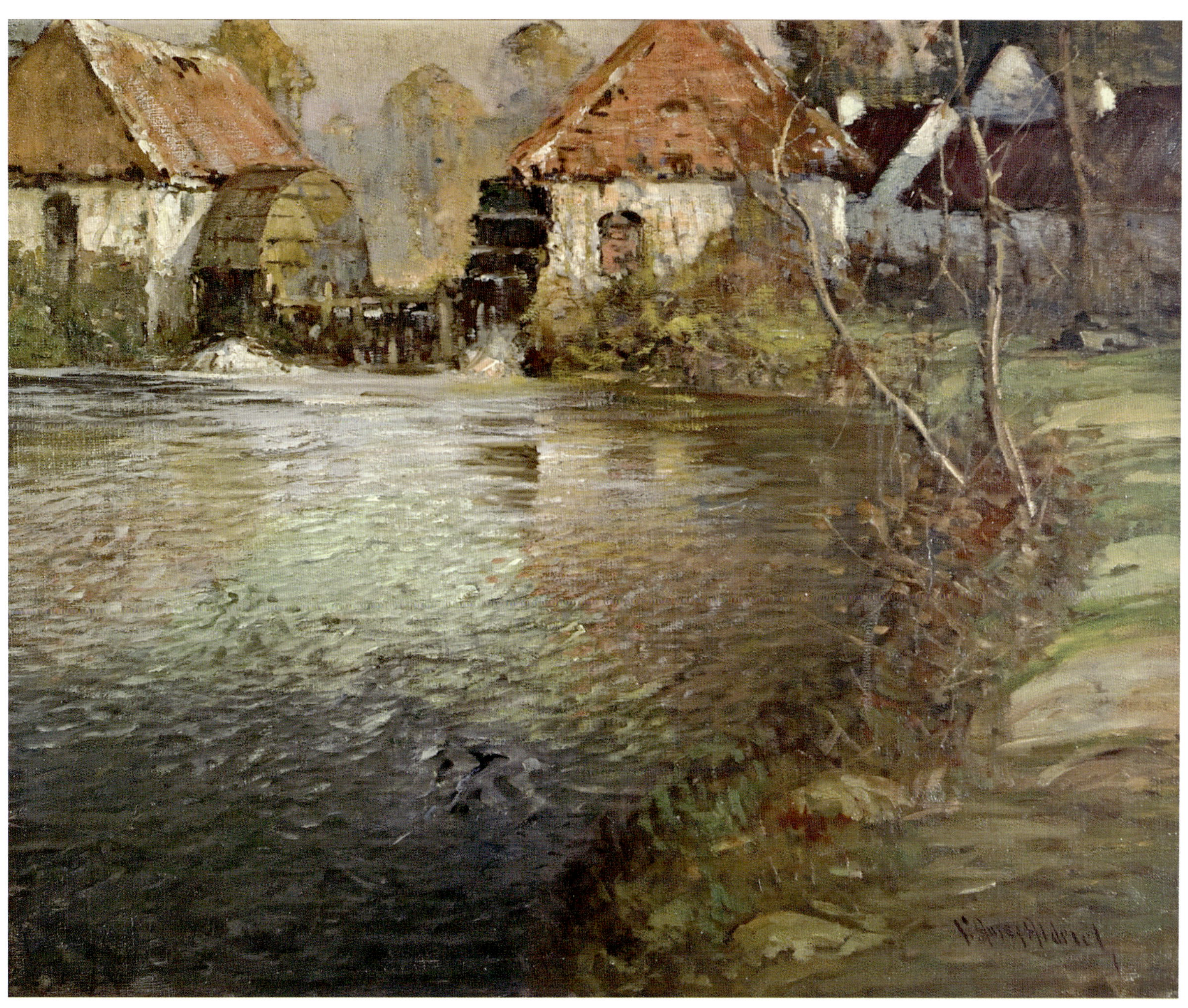

PLATE 9

Untitled (double mill), undated

Oil on canvas, 25 × 30 inches

Collection of Mark Forrest West

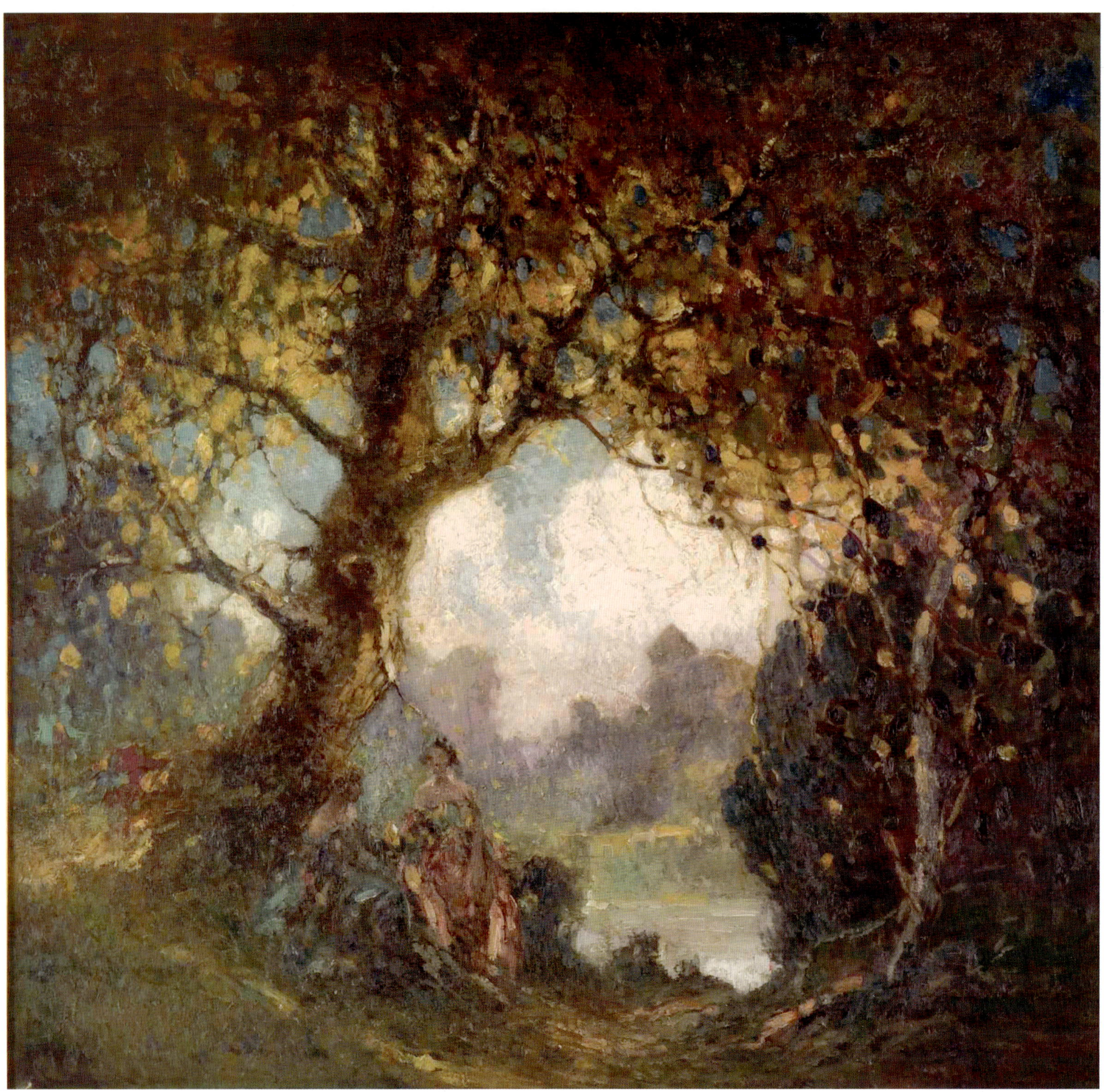

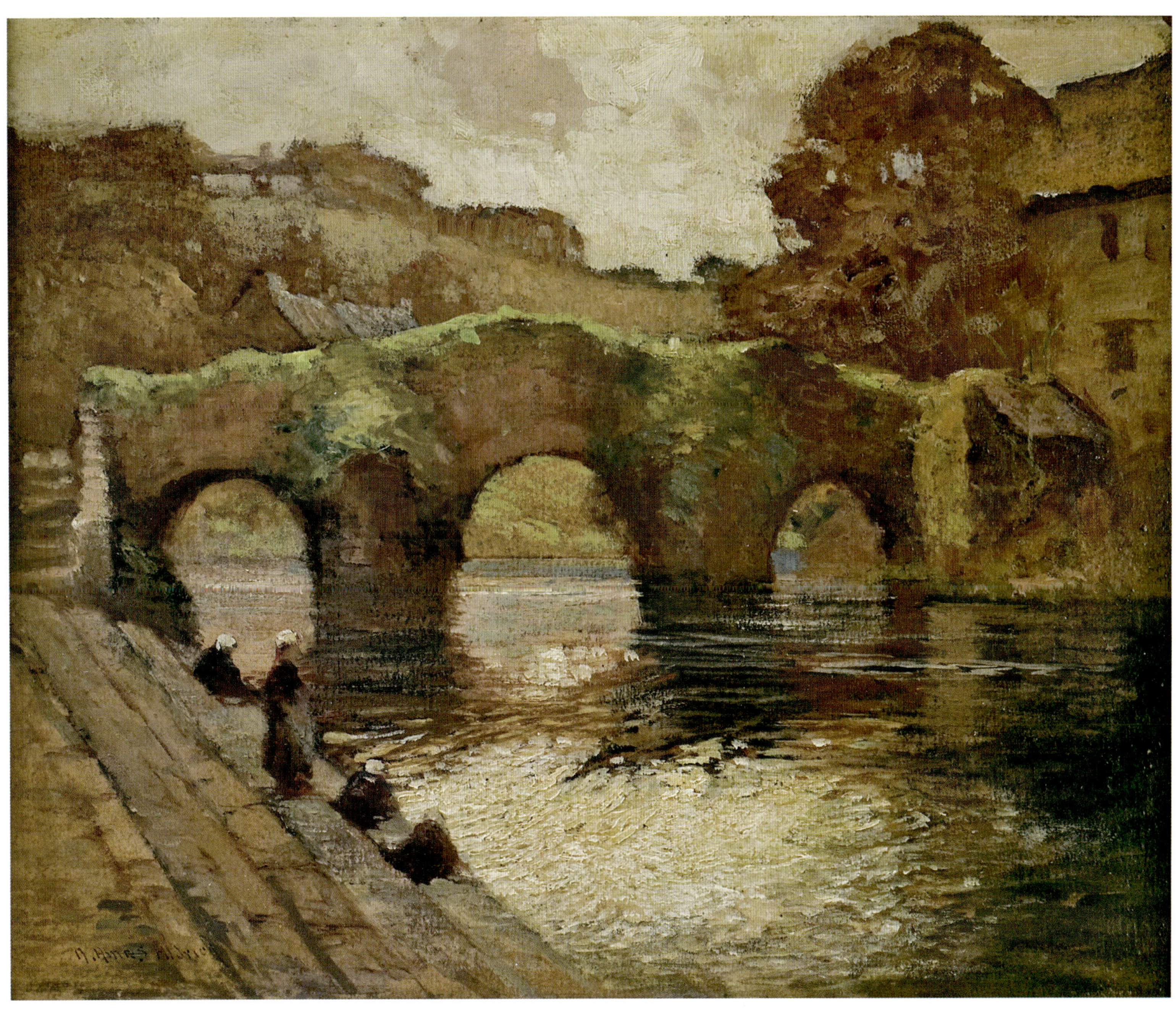

PLATE 10 {FACING}
Indian Summer, undated
Oil on canvas, 39 × 39 inches
Sioux City Art Center Permanent Collection, 968.03, Gift of Edna Weld Kliwer

PLATE 11
Untitled (bridge at Quimperlé), undated
Oil on board, 10 × 12 inches
Private Collection

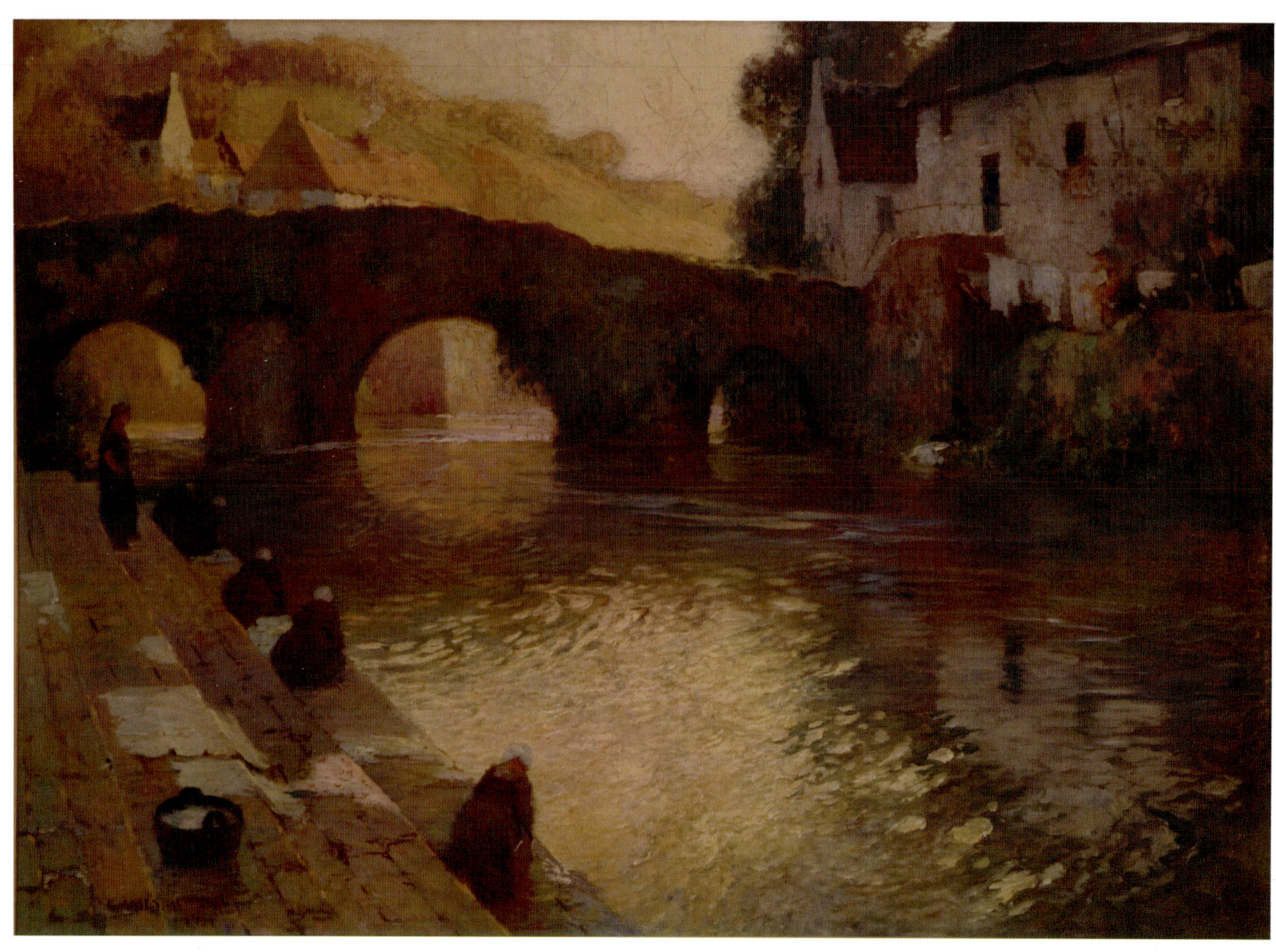

PLATE 12
Washerwomen of Quimperlé, 1921
Oil on canvas, 24 × 36 inches
Private Collection

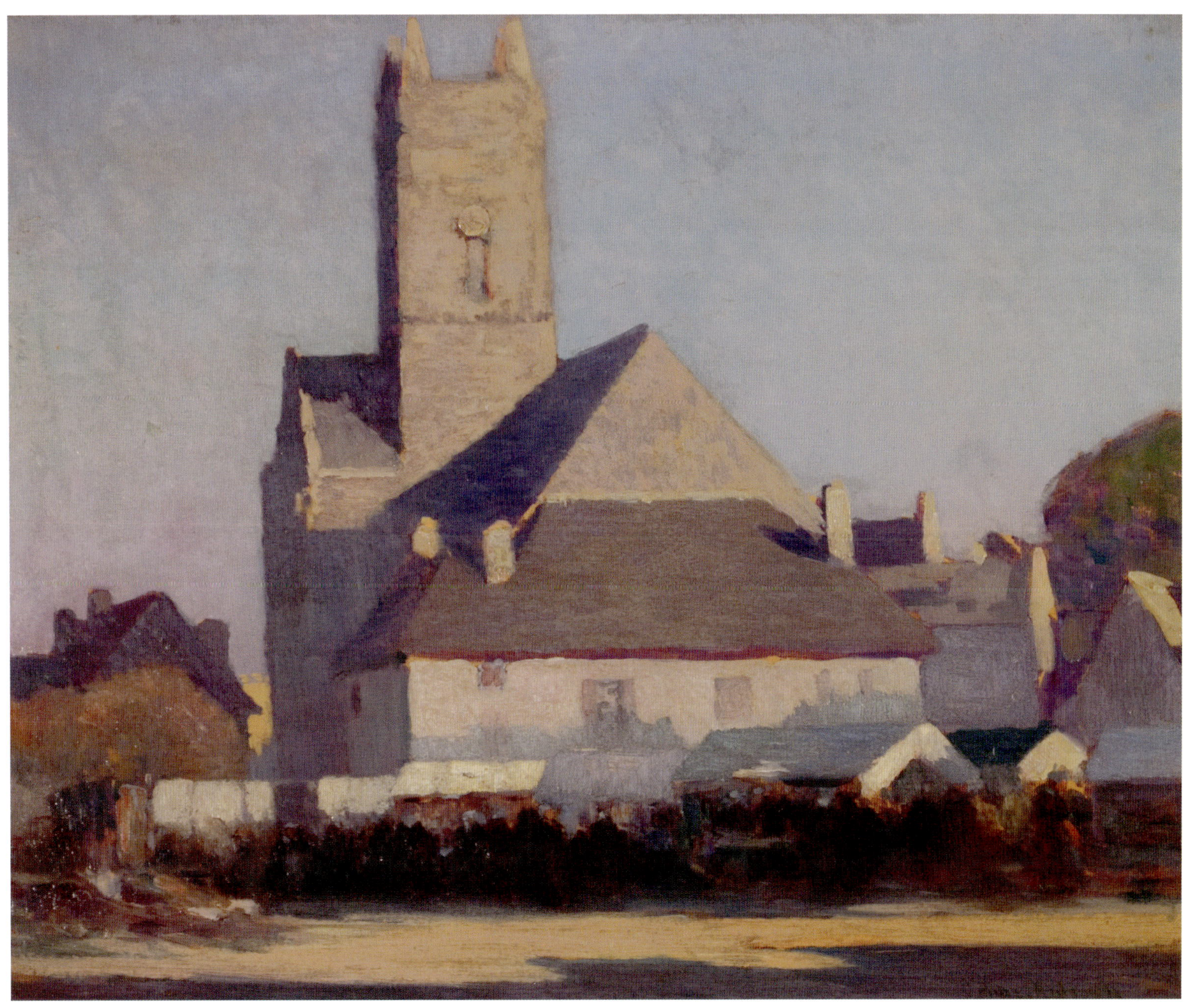

PLATE 13
Untitled (European church scene), undated
Oil on board, 20 × 24 inches
South Bend Museum of Art, Gift of Mary Anna Peacock Birdzell, 2000.1

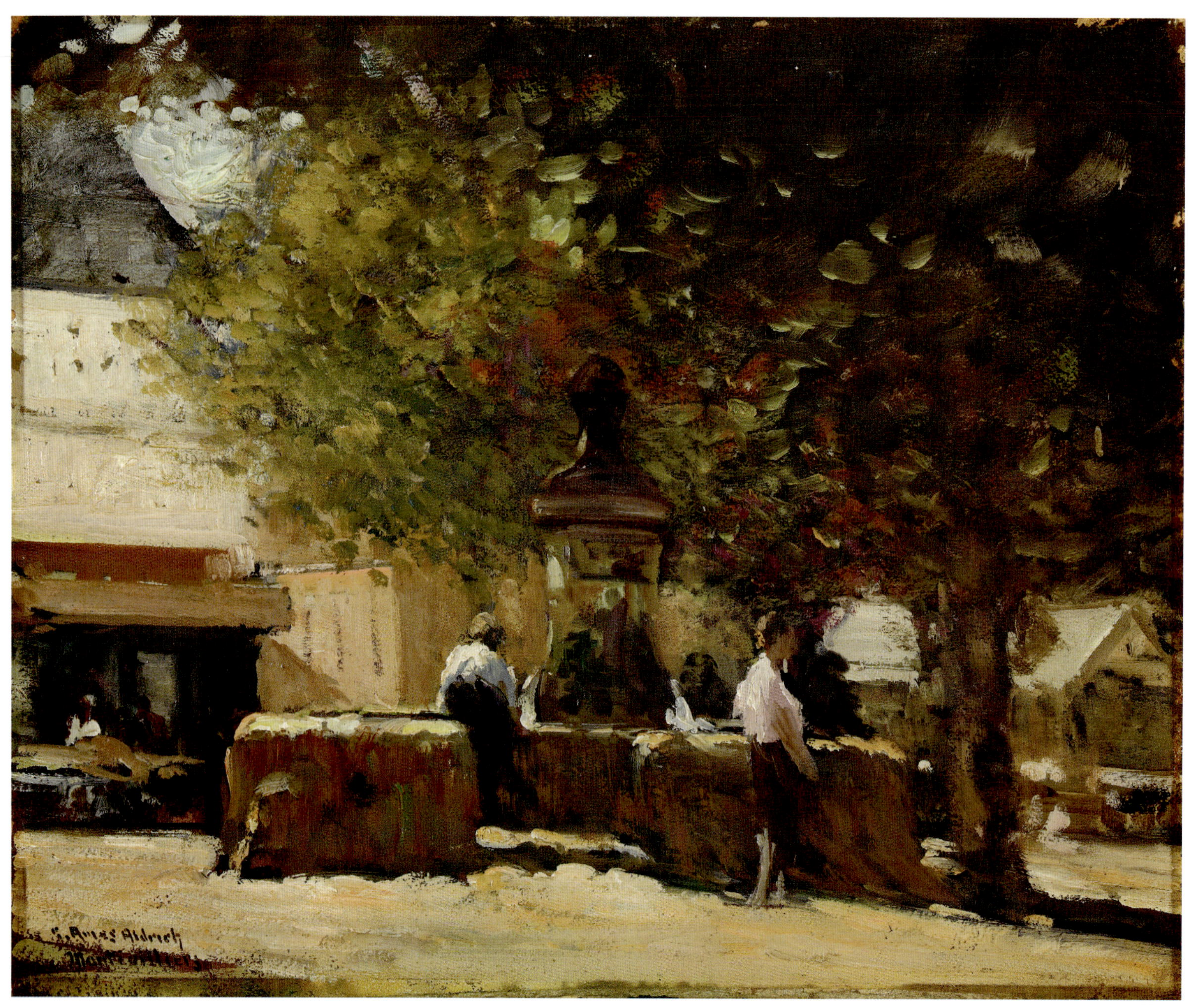

PLATE 14
Untitled (village fountain), undated
Oil on board, 14 × 16 inches
Collection of Richard and Jean Dennen

PLATE 15 {FACING}
Untitled (village rooftops), undated
Oil on canvas, 24 × 20 inches
Collection of Richard and Jean Dennen

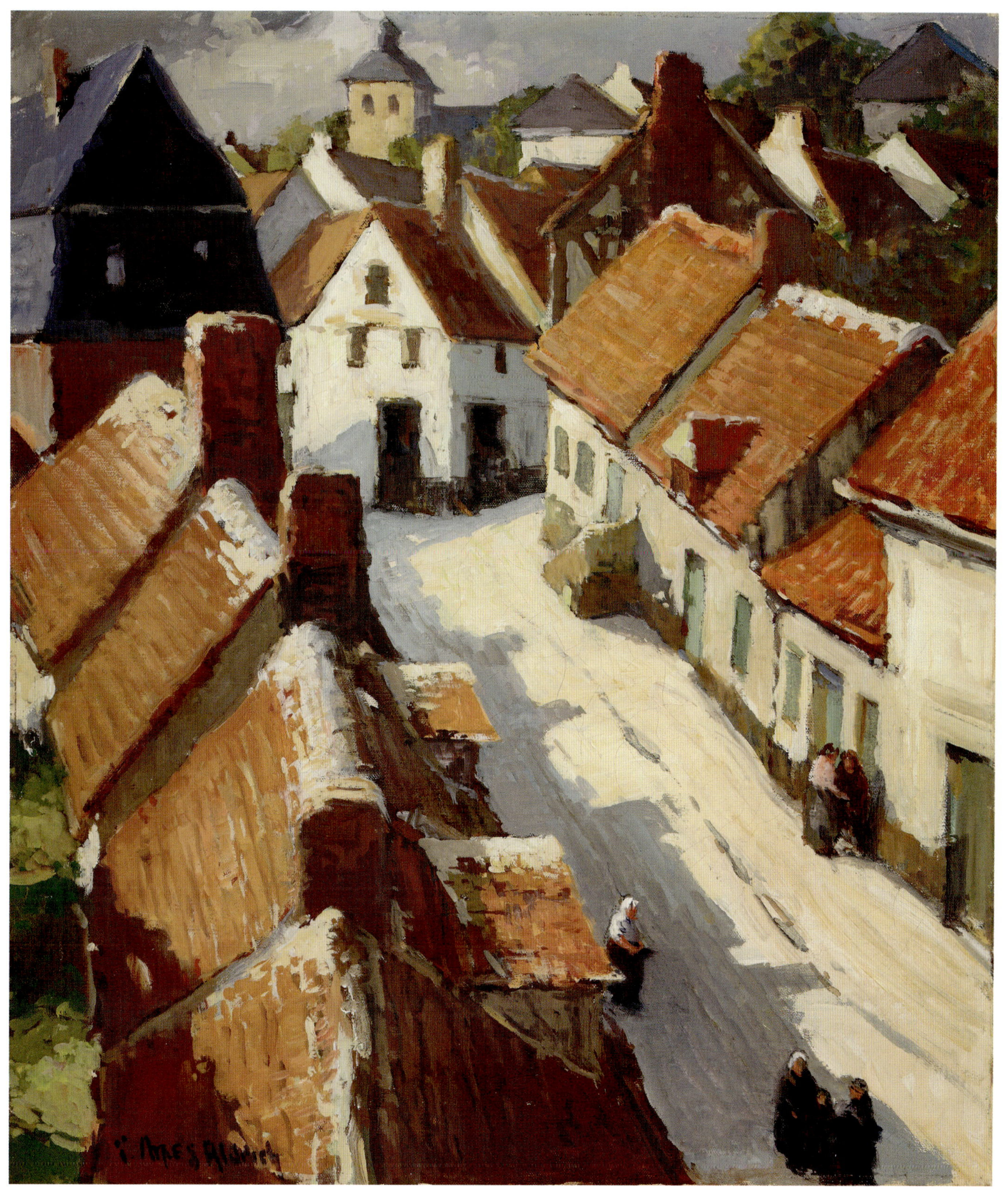

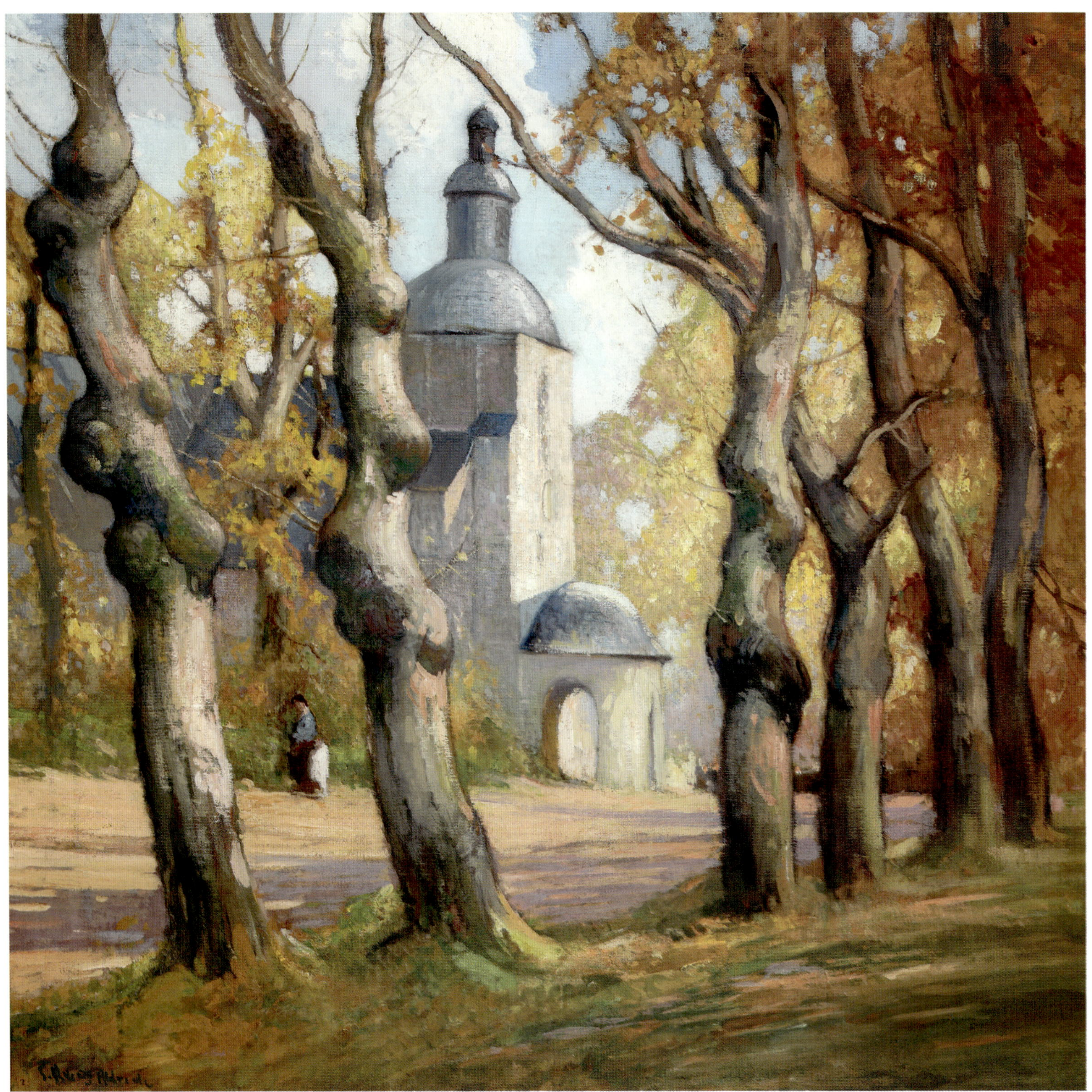

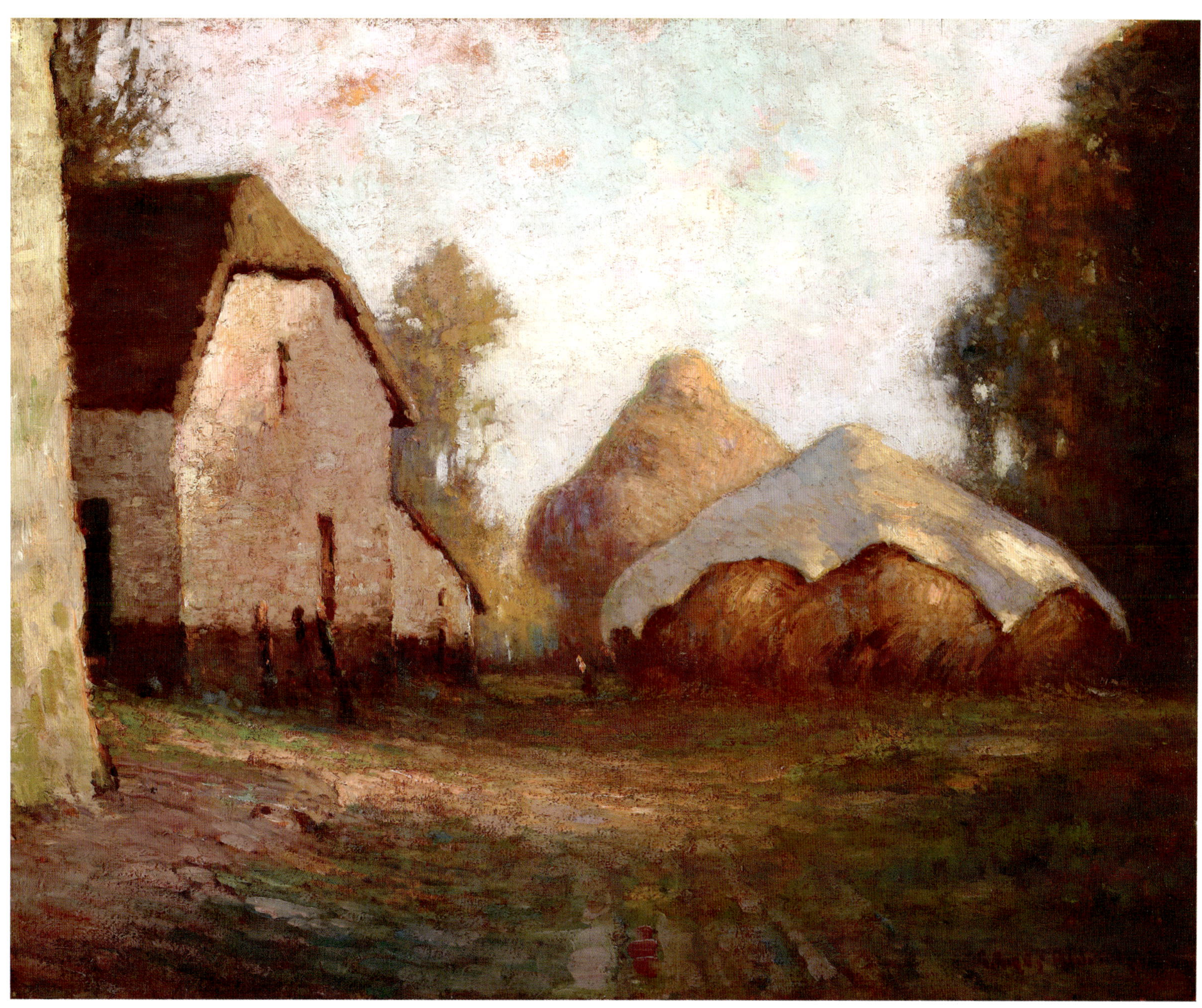

PLATE 16 {FACING}
Sailors' Church Hon Fleur, undated
Oil on canvas, 36 × 36 inches
Collection of the Charles S. Hayes Family

PLATE 17
Untitled (haystacks), undated
Oil on board, 20 × 24 inches
Private Collection

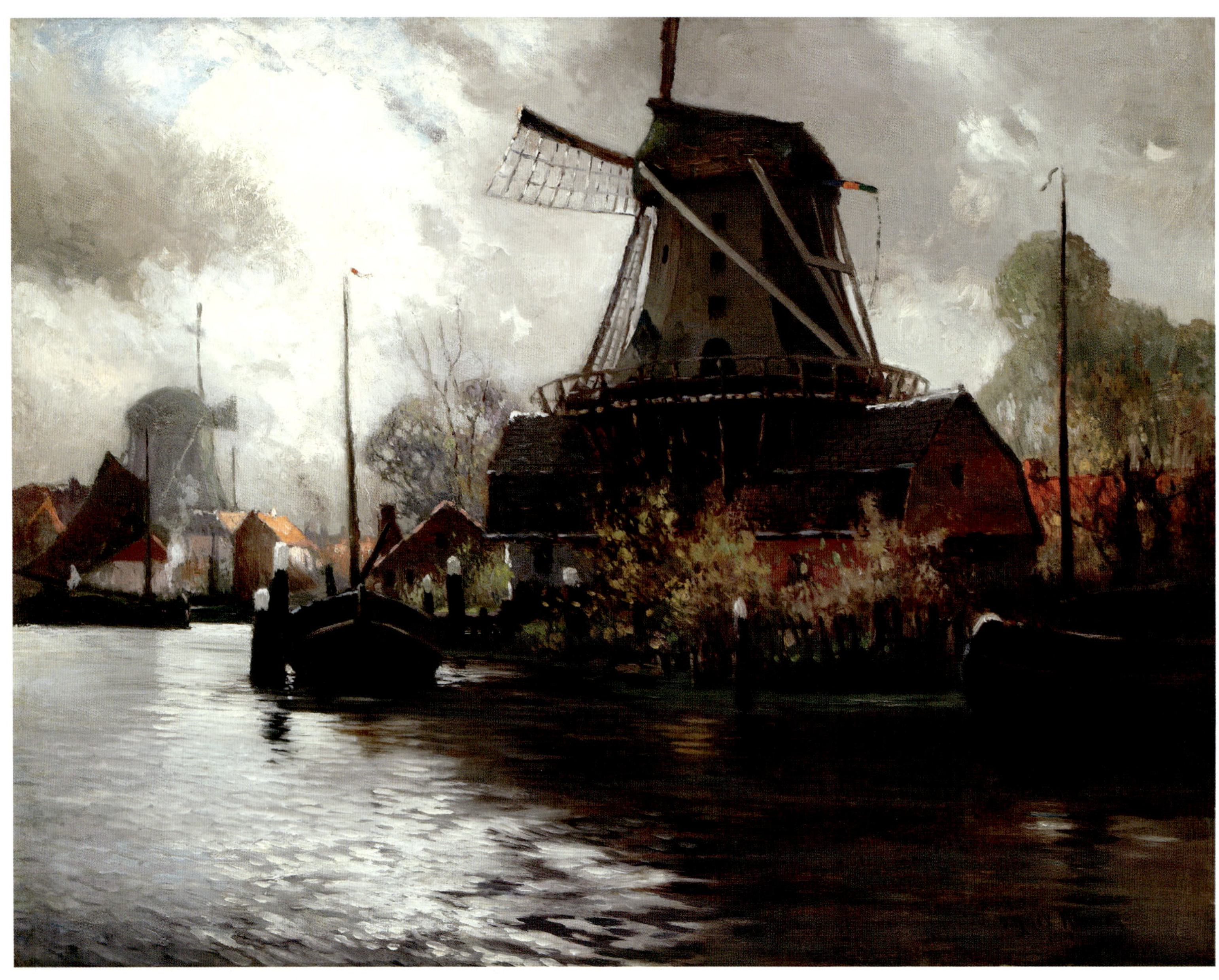

PLATE 18
Untitled (windmill on canal), undated
Oil on canvas, 24 × 30 inches
Private Collection

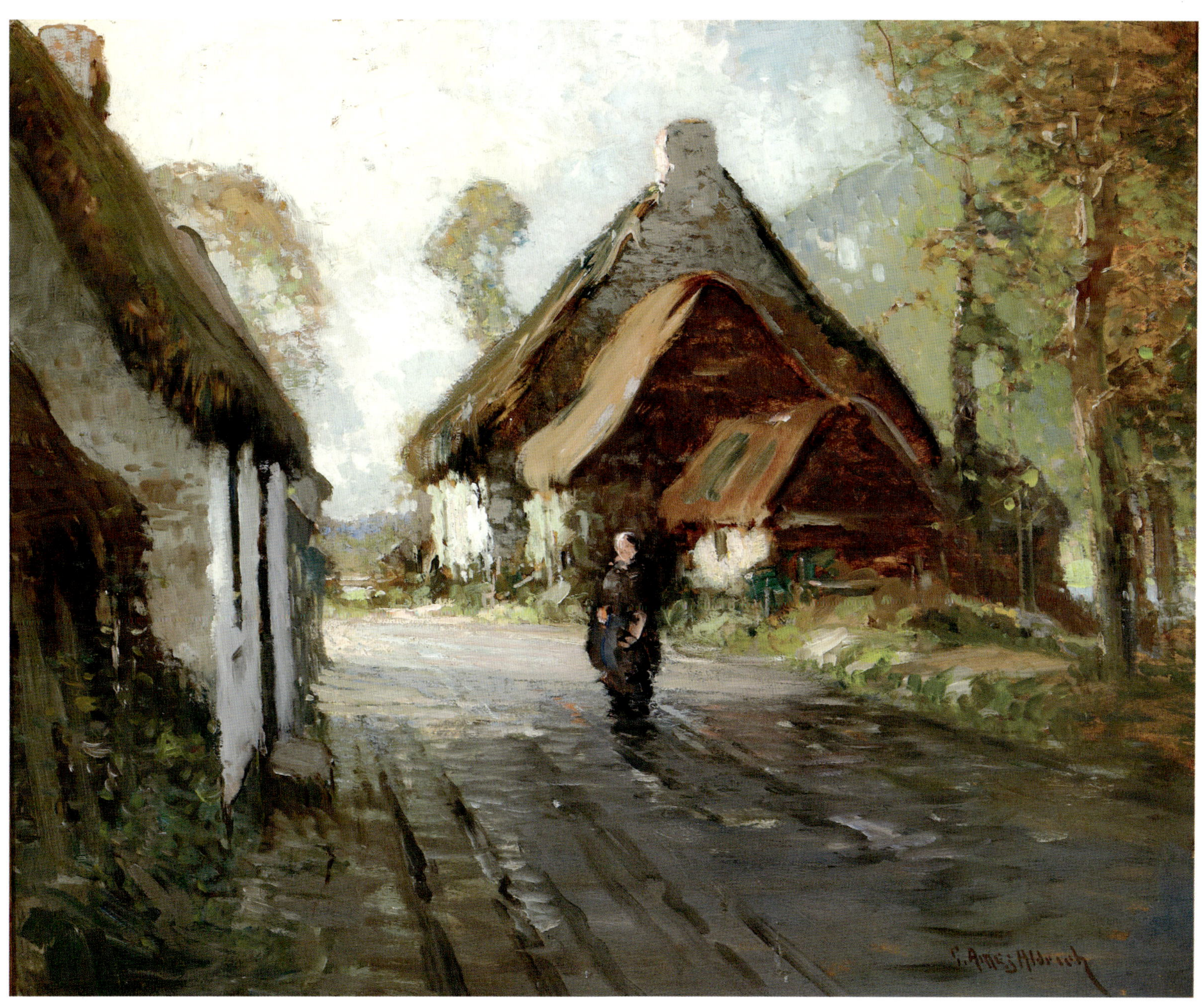

PLATE 19
Untitled (Rysoord, Holland), undated
Oil on board, 24 × 30 inches
Collection of the Charles S. Hayes Family

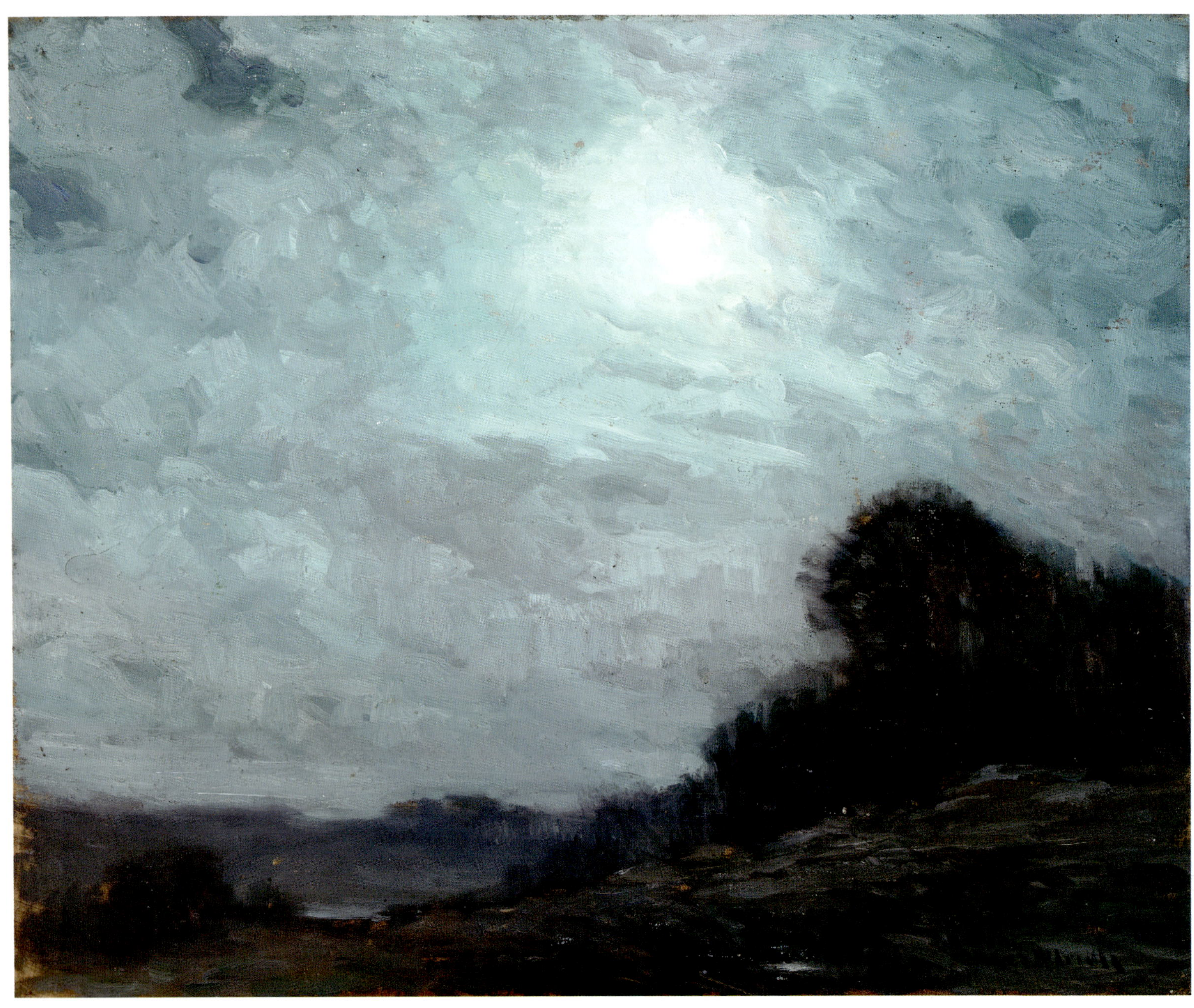

PLATE 20
Untitled (nocturne landscape), undated
Oil on linen, 20 × 24 inches
Private Collection

PLATE 21 {FACING}
Untitled (nocturne church), undated
Oil on board, 24 × 24 inches
Collection of the Charles S. Hayes Family

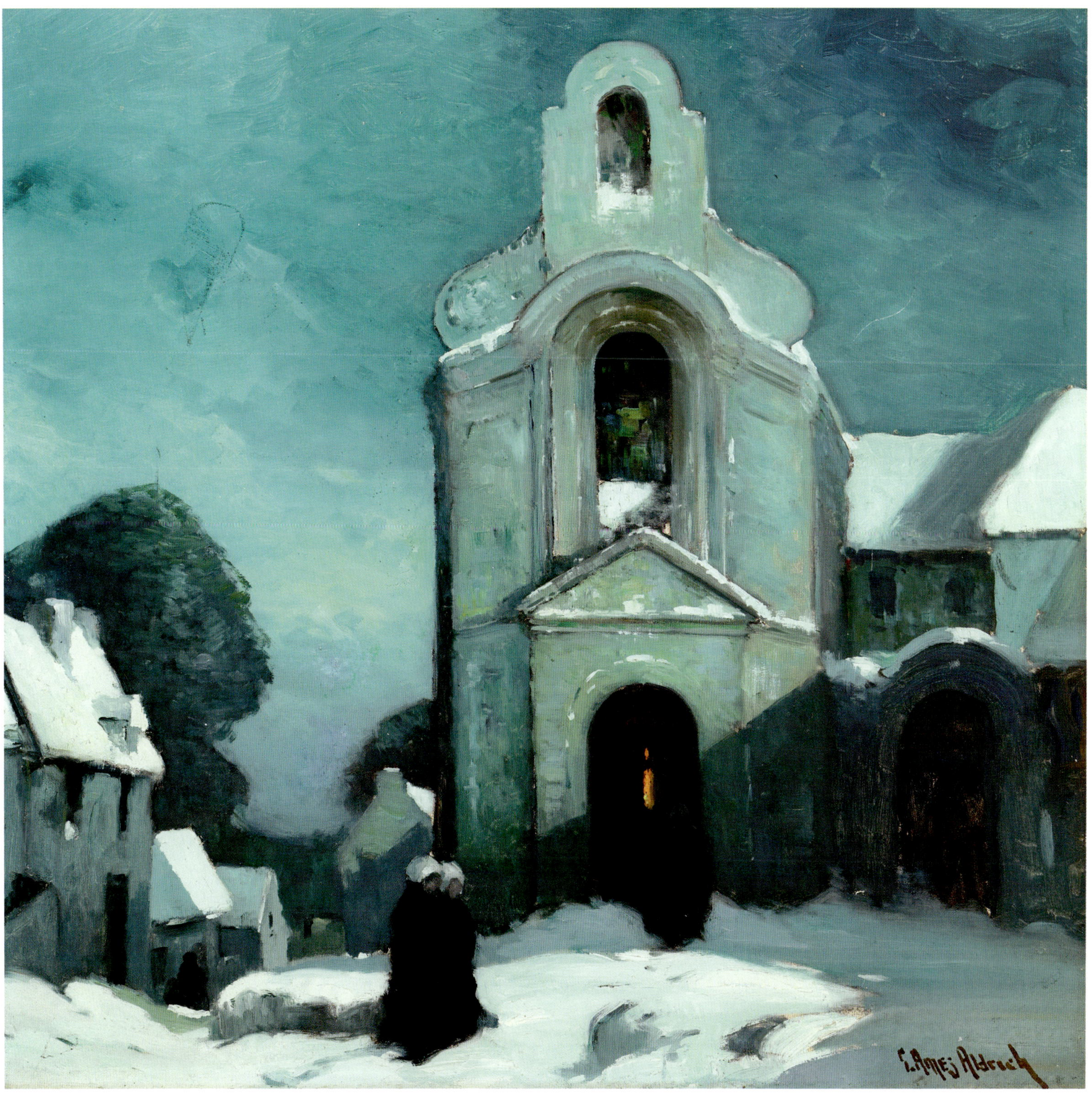
C. Ames Aldrich

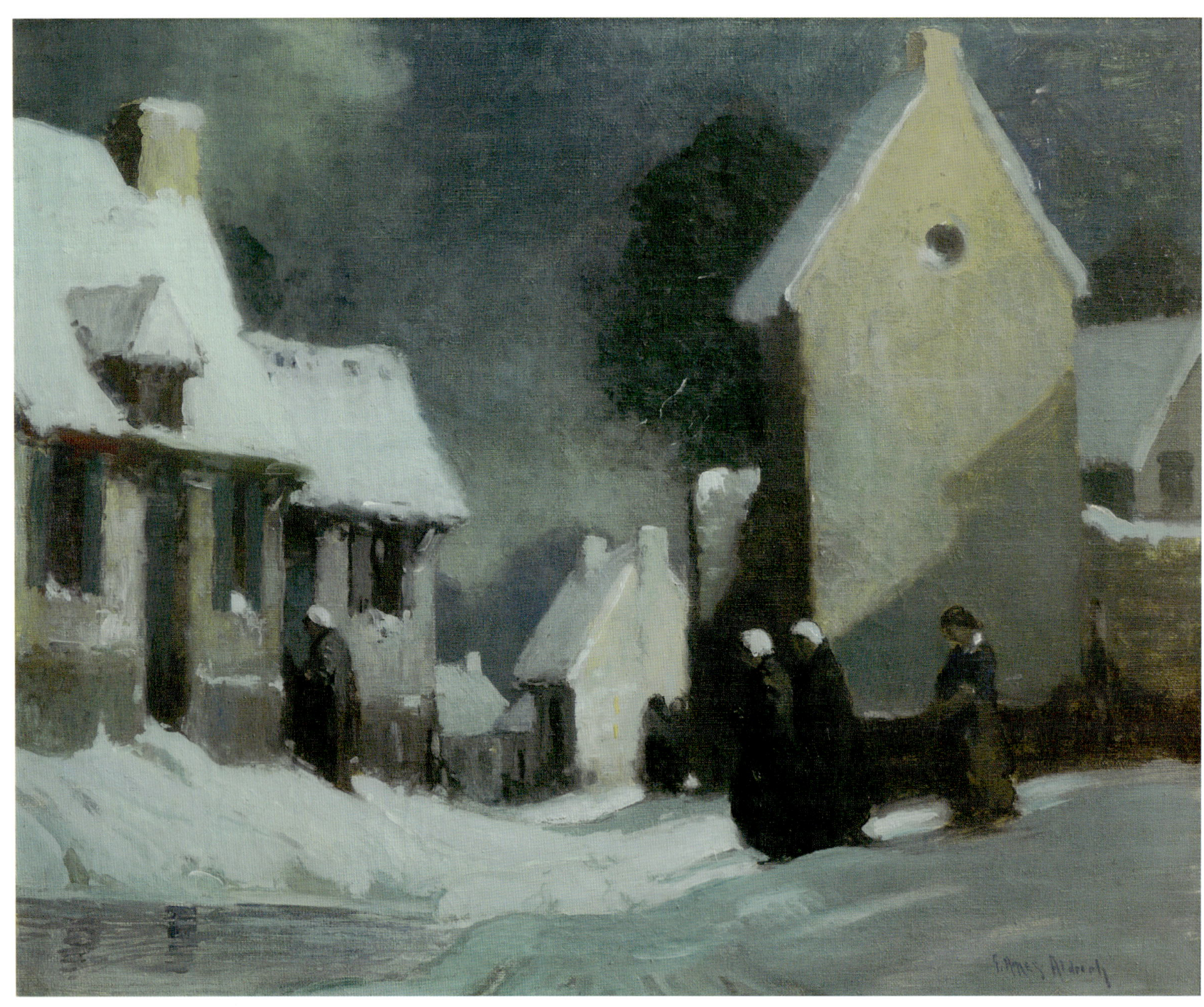

PLATE 22

French Village at Night, undated

Oil on canvas, 25 × 30 inches

Art Museum of Greater Lafayette, Gift of Robert L. and Ellen E. Haan, 1998.12

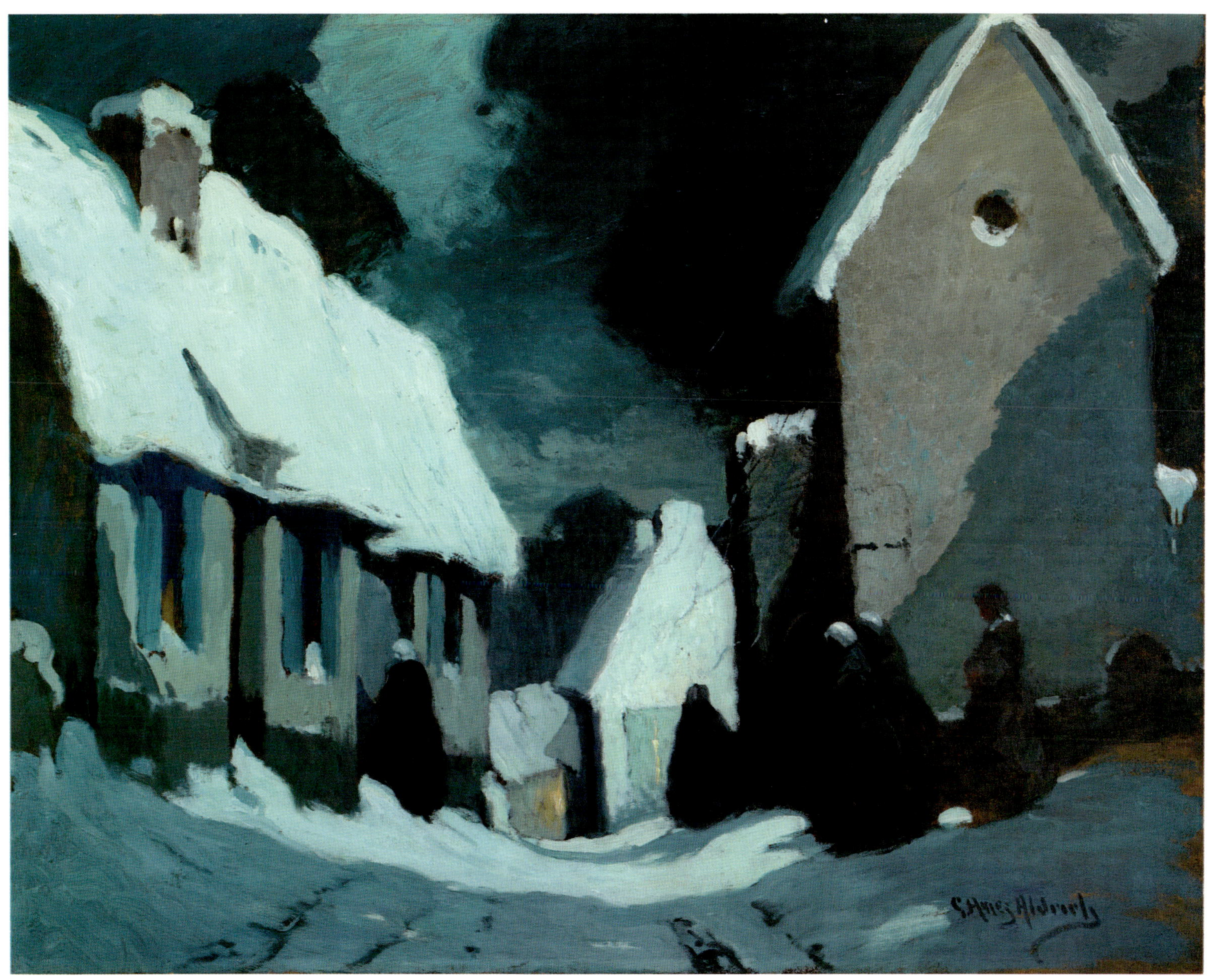

PLATE 23
Street Scene with Five Figures, undated
Oil on canvas, 32 × 40 inches
Permanent Collection, Snite Museum of Art, University of Notre Dame, Gift of the Estate of Catherine Slaughter, 1965.005.001

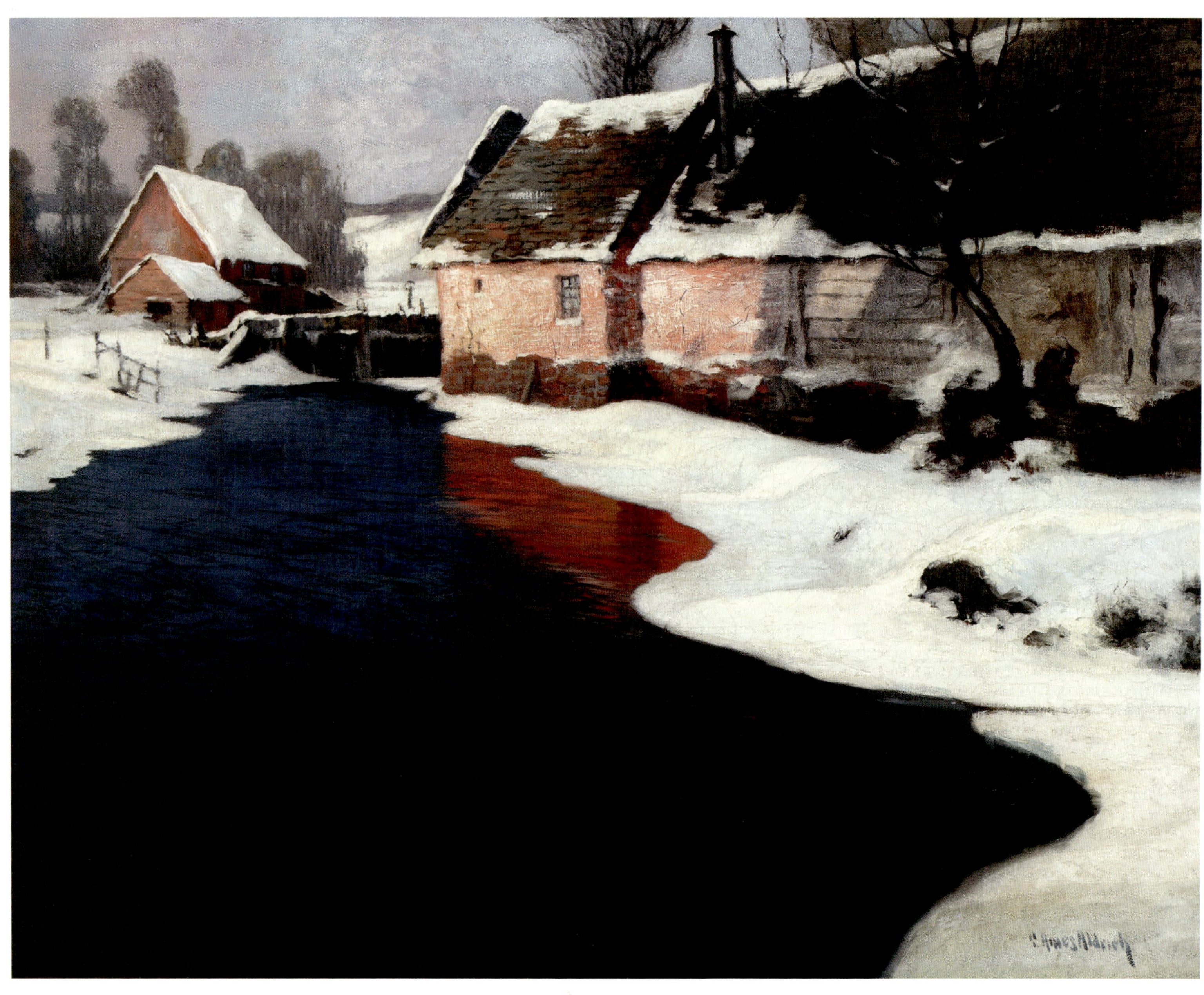

PLATE 24
Untitled (factory by river, winter), undated
Oil on canvas, 26 × 32 inches
Collection of the Charles S. Hayes Family

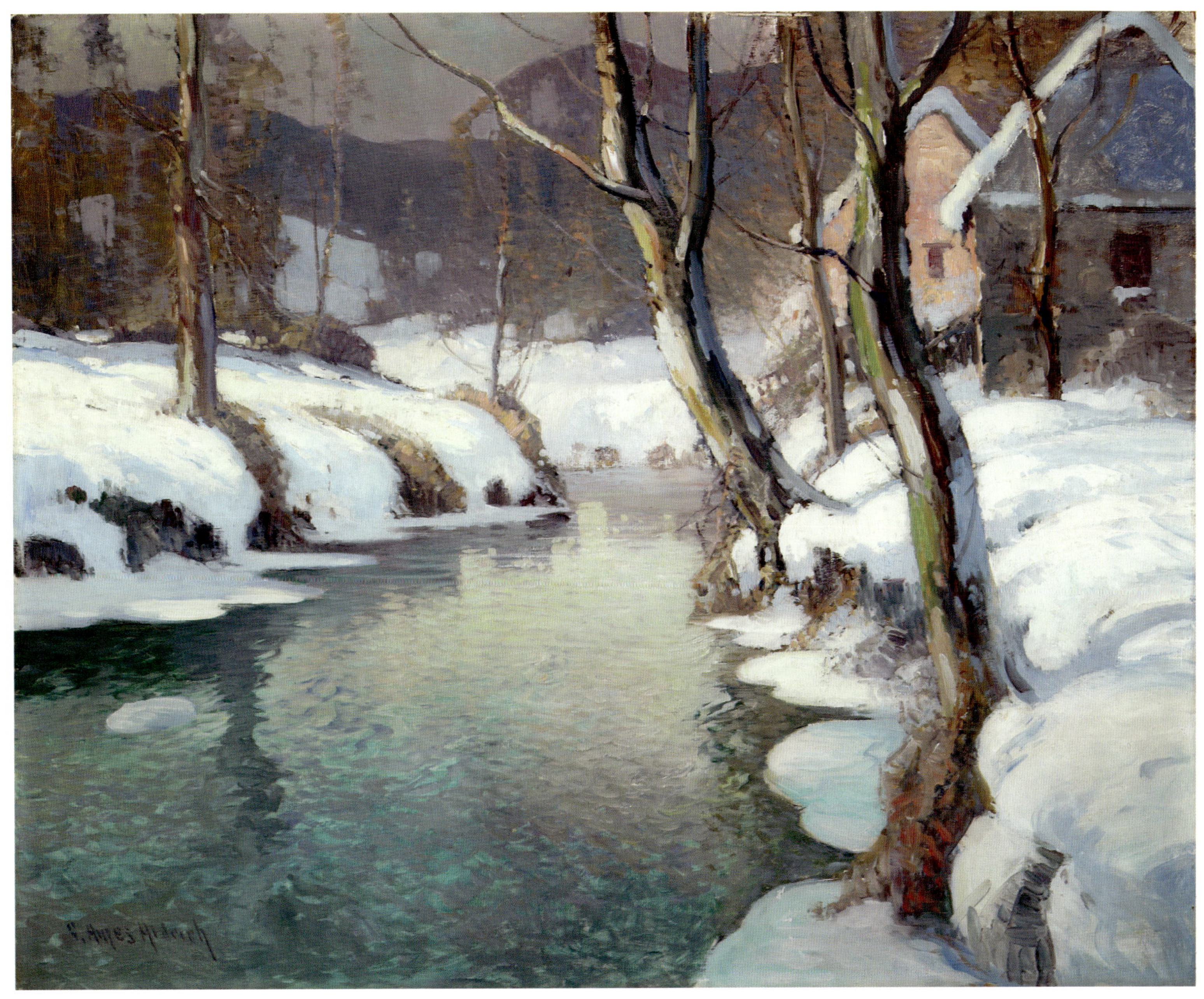

PLATE 25
Untitled (winter river), undated
Oil on board, 25 × 30 inches
Collection of the Charles S. Hayes Family

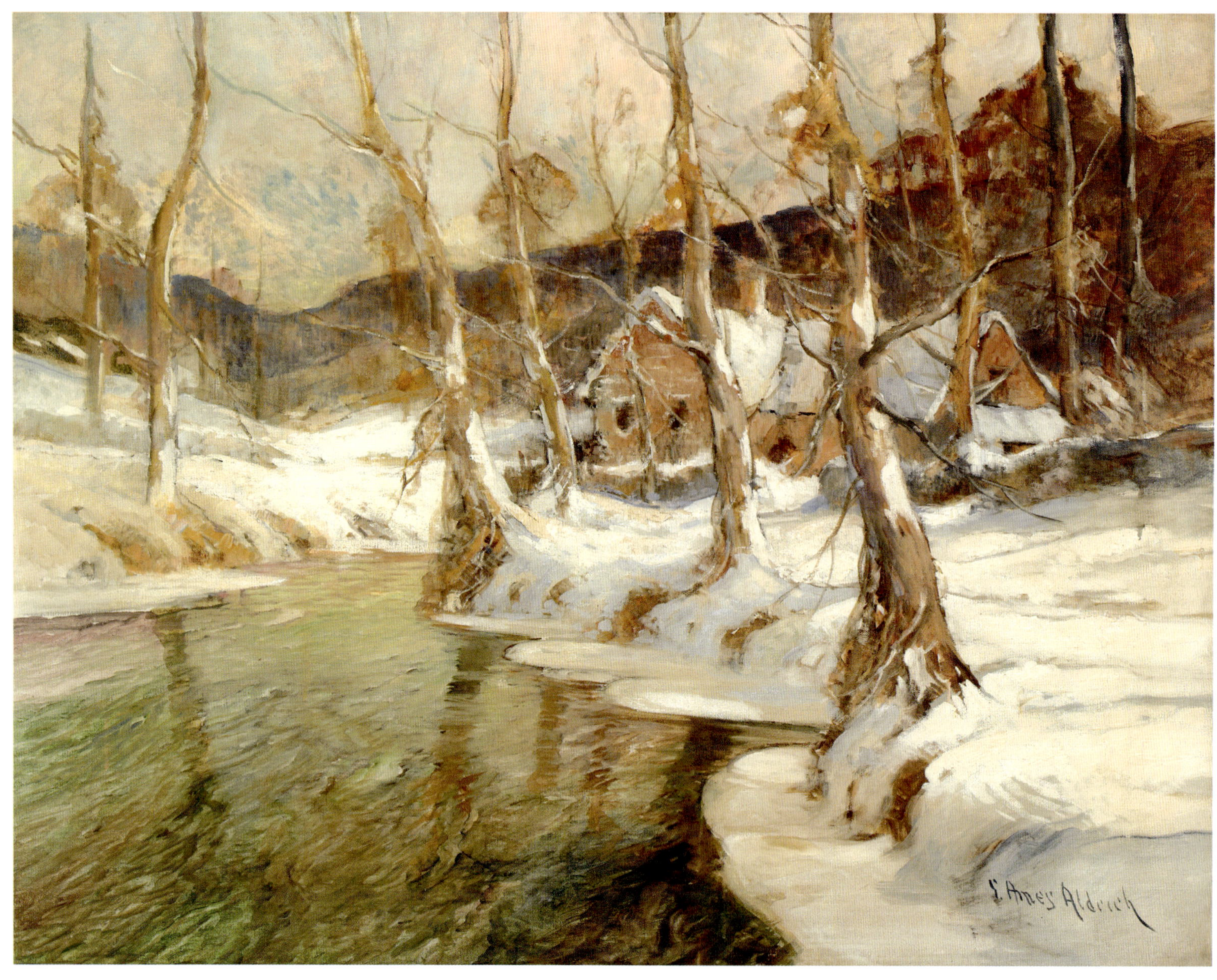

PLATE 26

Untitled (cottages by river, winter), undated

Oil on canvas, 40 × 50 inches

Private Collection

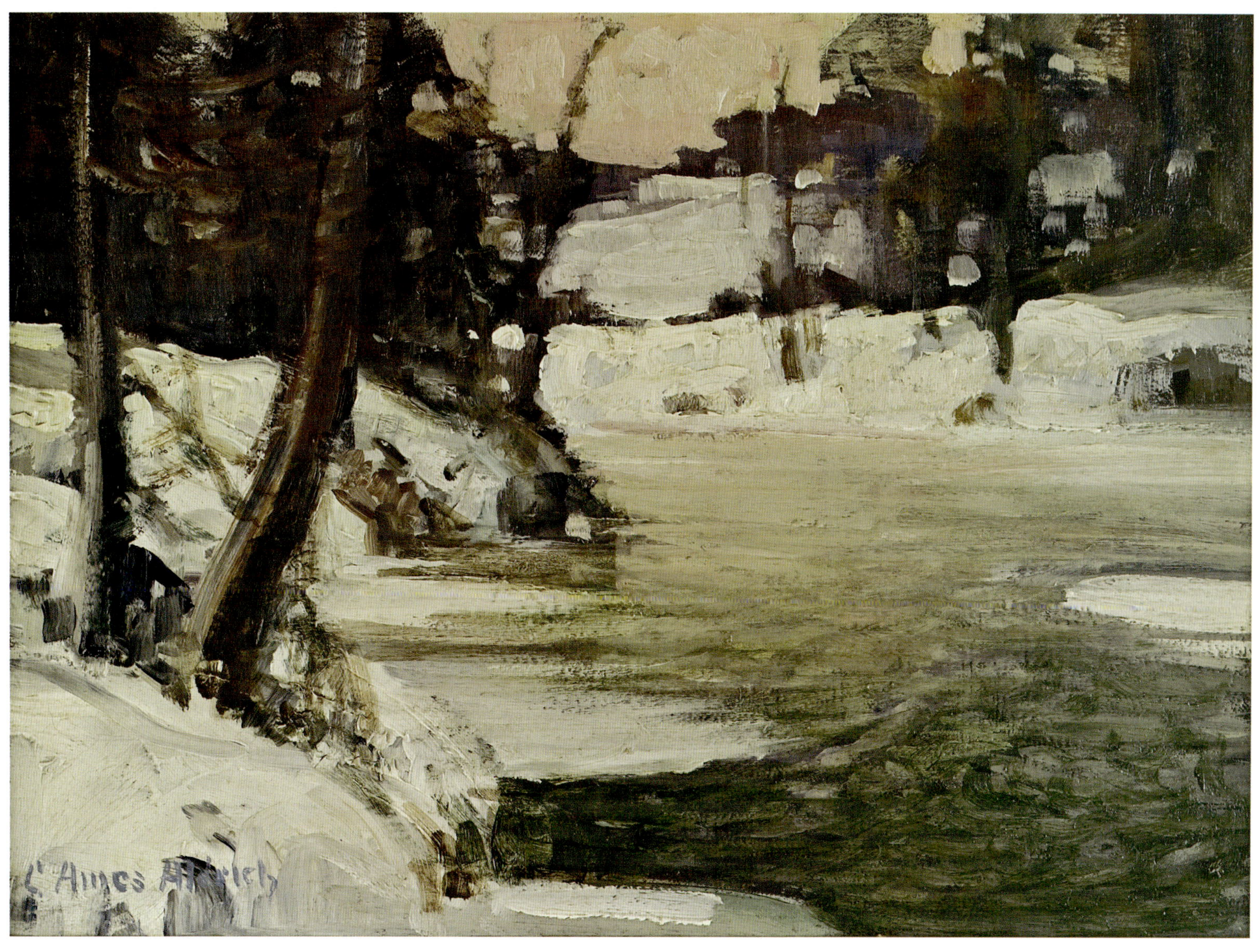

PLATE 27
Untitled (St. Joe River), undated
Oil on board, 9 × 12 inches
Private Collection

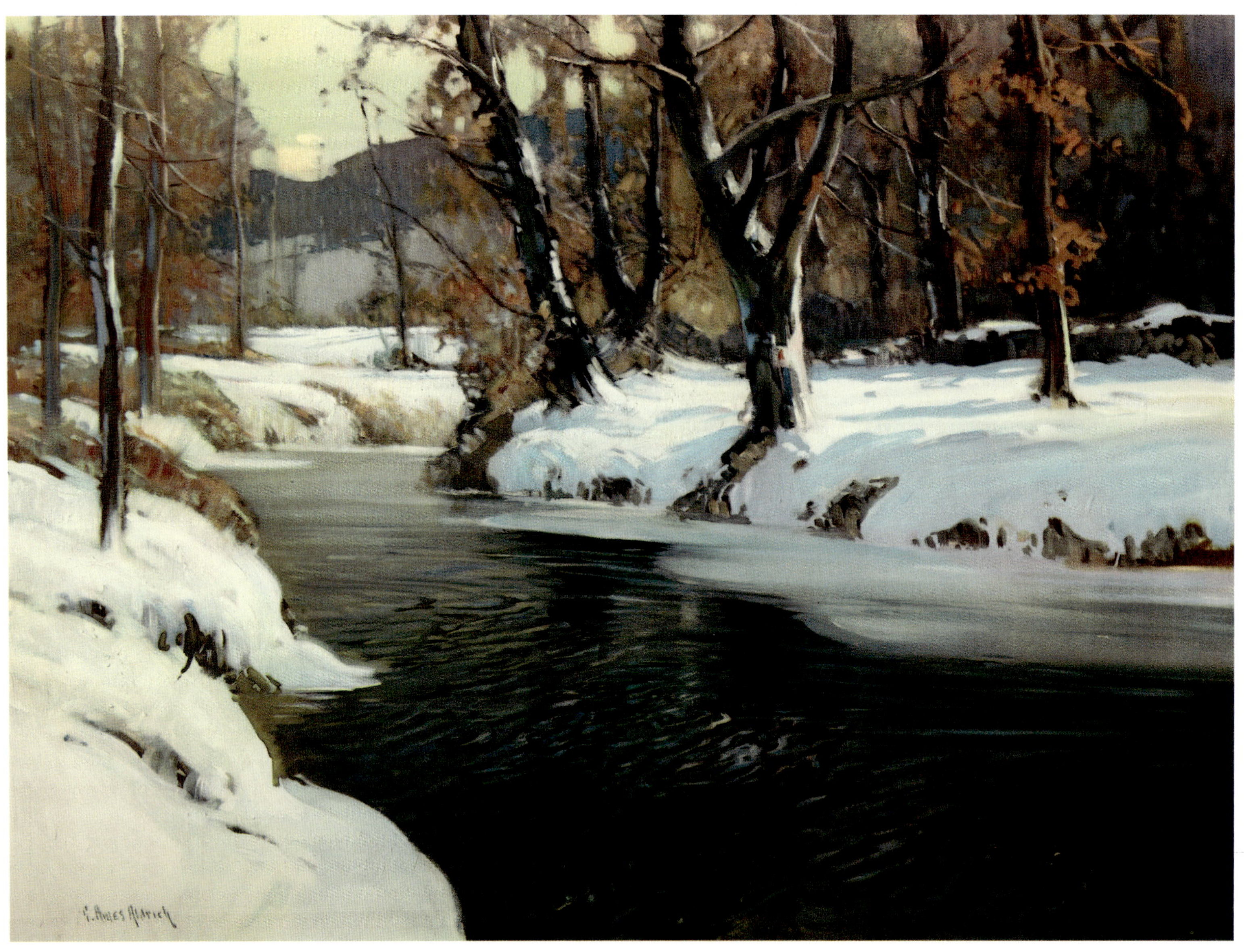

PLATE 28

Winter's Glory (promotional giveaway for Iodent toothpaste), ca. 1932

Offset lithograph on paper, image: 12 ¾ × 16 ¾ inches, paper: 13 ¼ × 17 ¼ inches

Private Collection

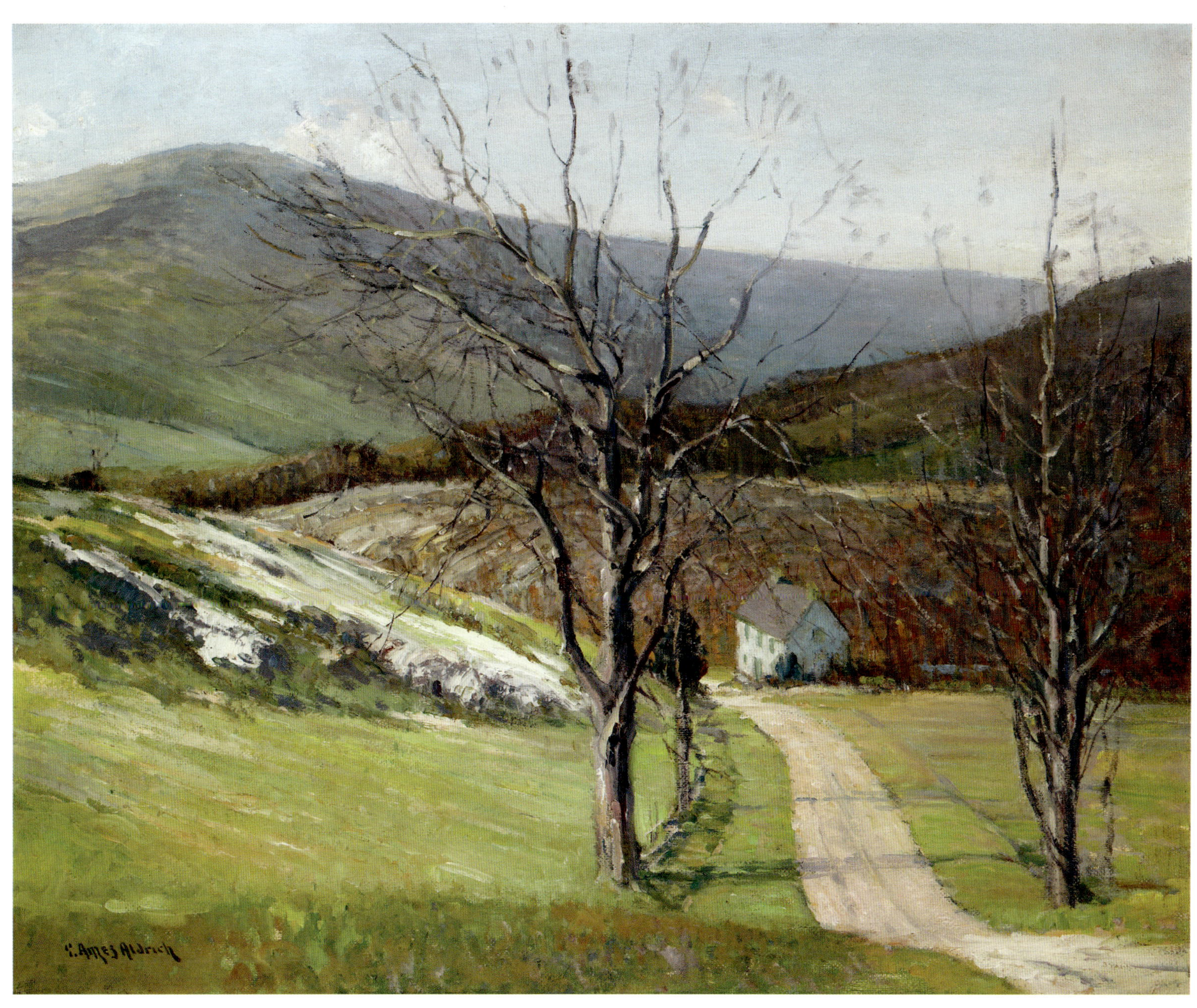

PLATE 29
Untitled (house along road in valley), undated
Oil on board, 25 × 30 inches
Collection of the Charles S. Hayes Family

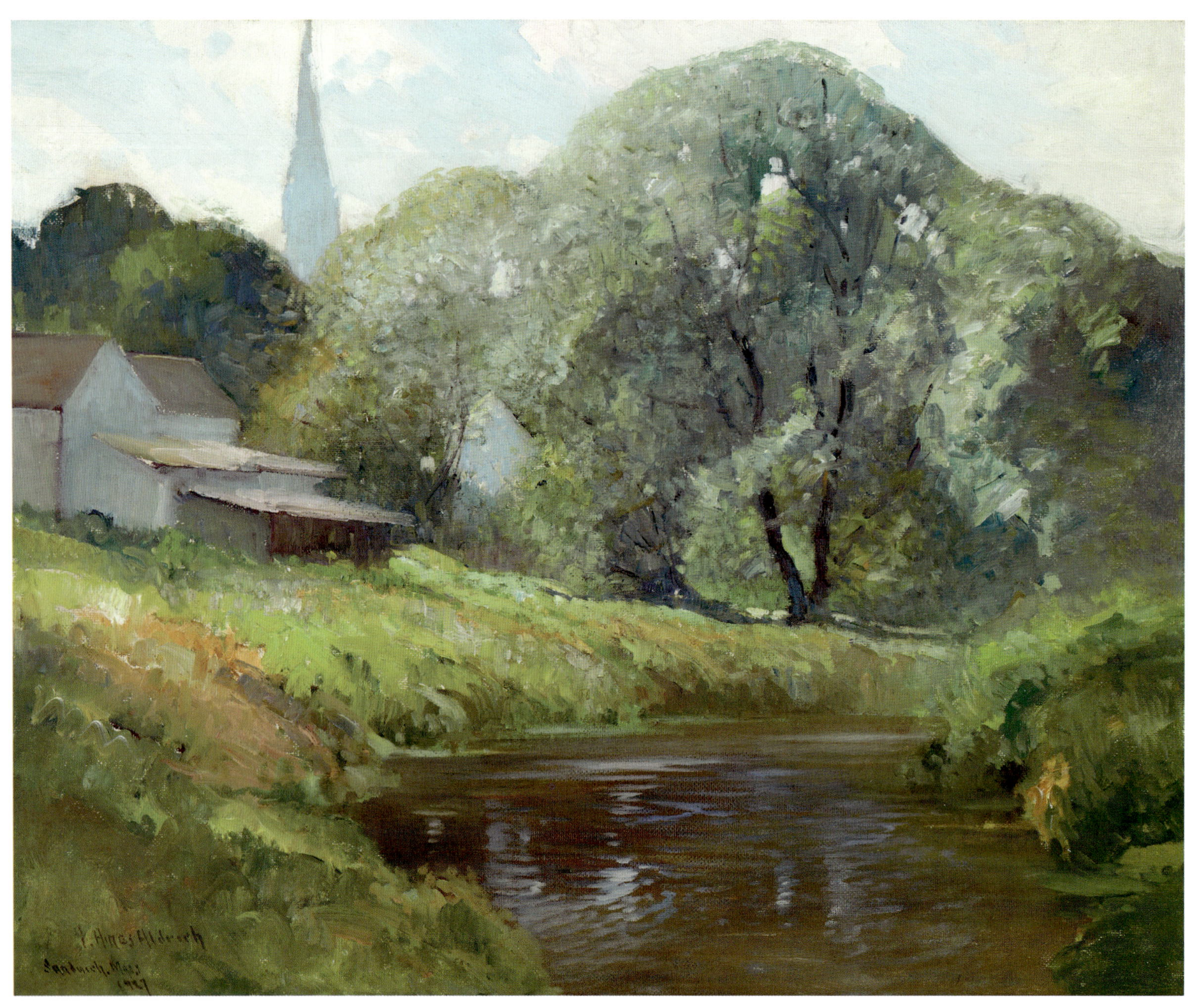

PLATE 30

Untitled (Sandwich, Massachusetts), 1921

Oil on board, 24 × 30 inches

Collection of the Charles S. Hayes Family

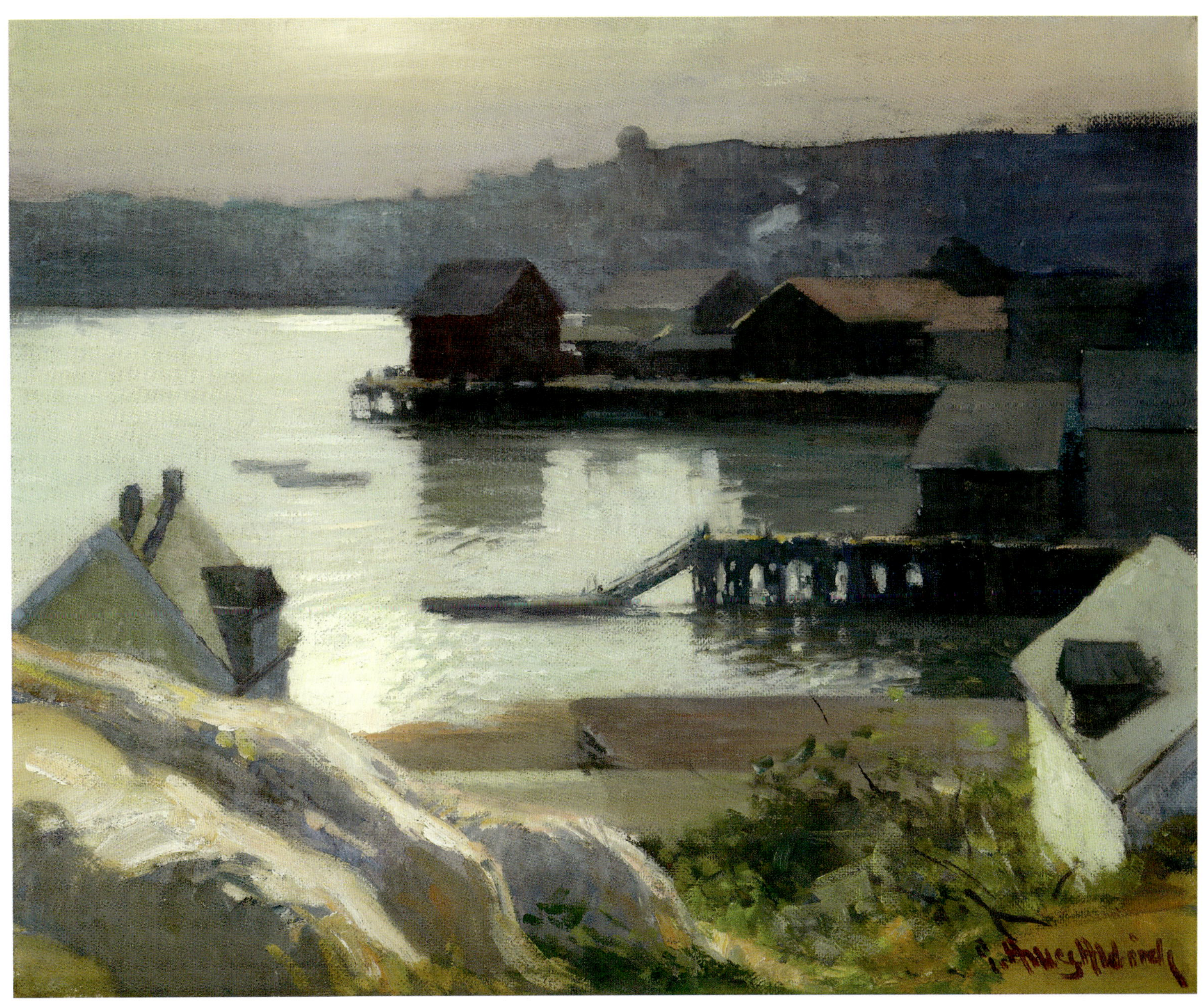

PLATE 31
Untitled (Gloucester scene), undated
Oil on board, 19 ½ × 23 ½ inches
Private Collection

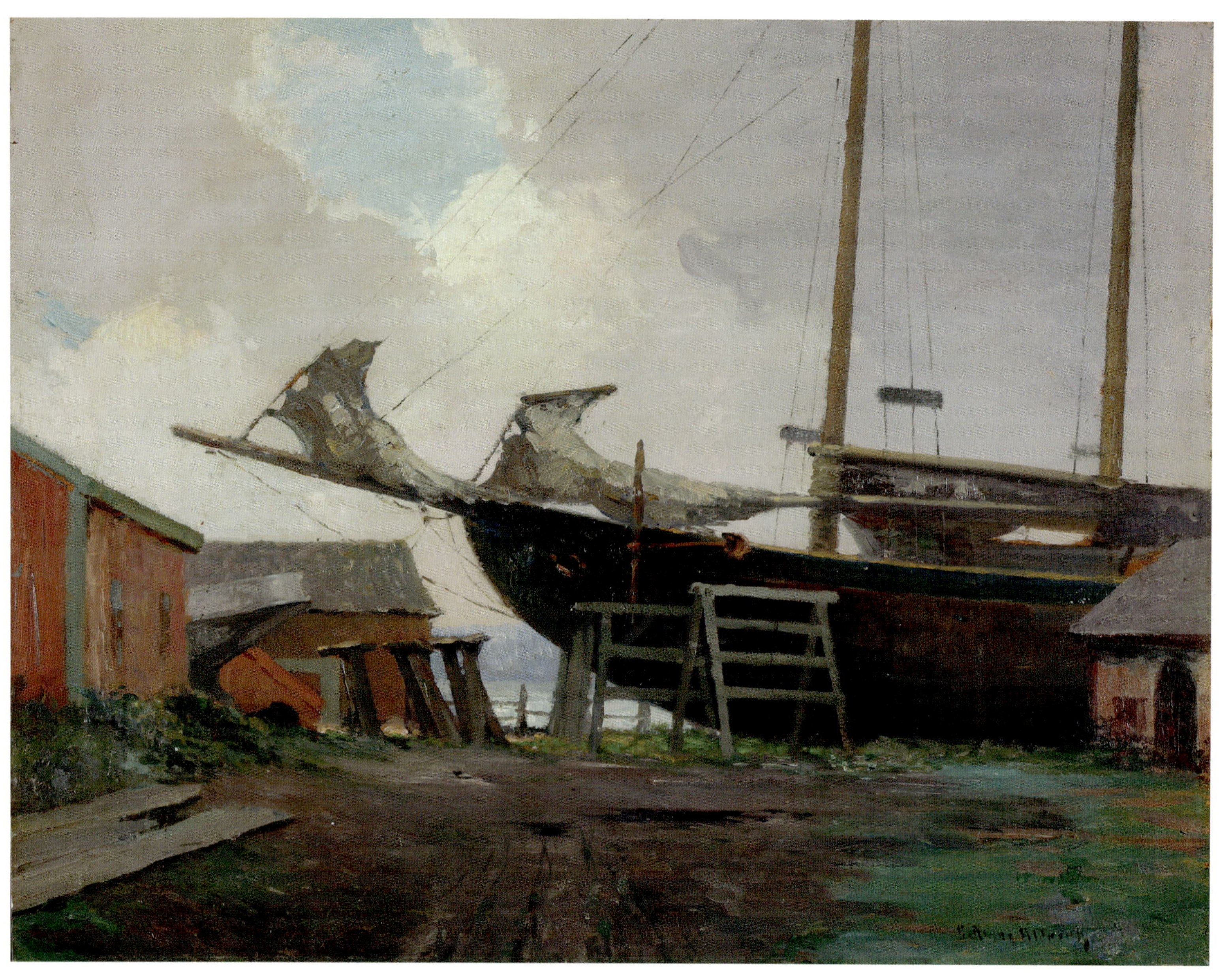

PLATE 32

Untitled (dry dock), undated

Oil on board, 23 × 29 inches

Collection of Martin and Deborah Radecki

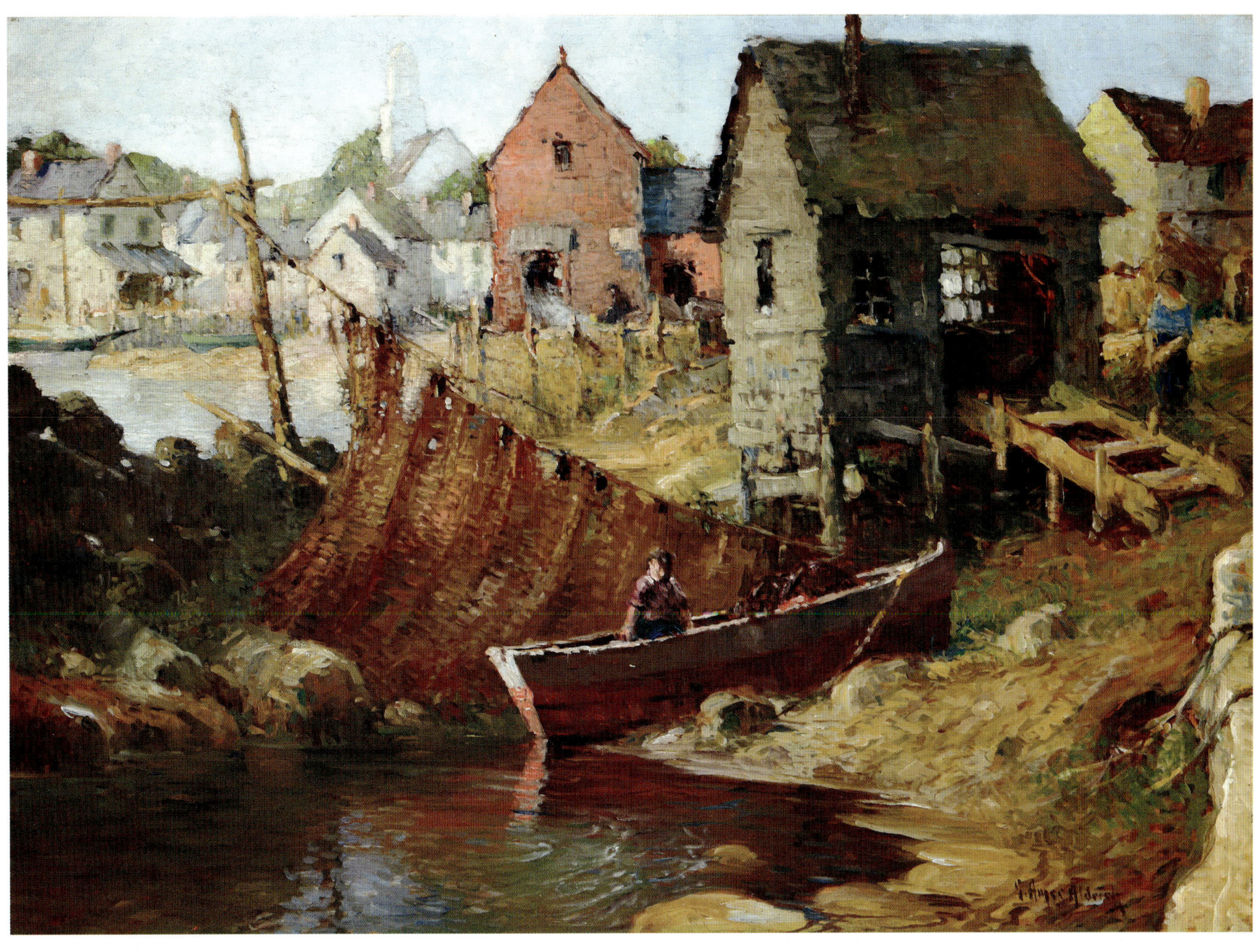

PLATE 33
Untitled (possibly Rockport, Massachusetts), undated
Oil on board, 30 × 40 inches
Collection of Elgin Mental Health Center

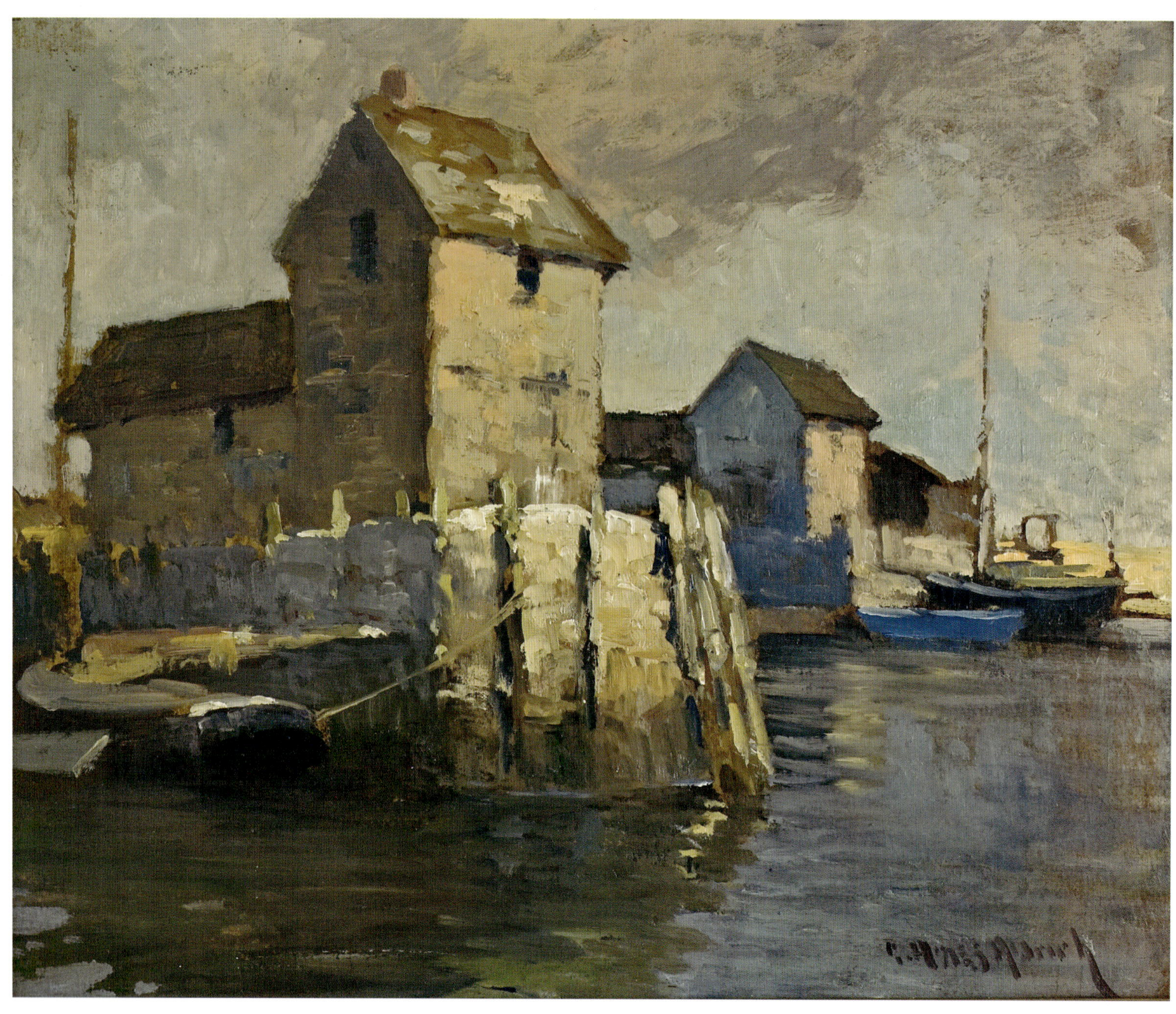

PLATE 34
Untitled (Maine harbor scene), undated
Oil on board, 12 × 14 inches
Private Collection

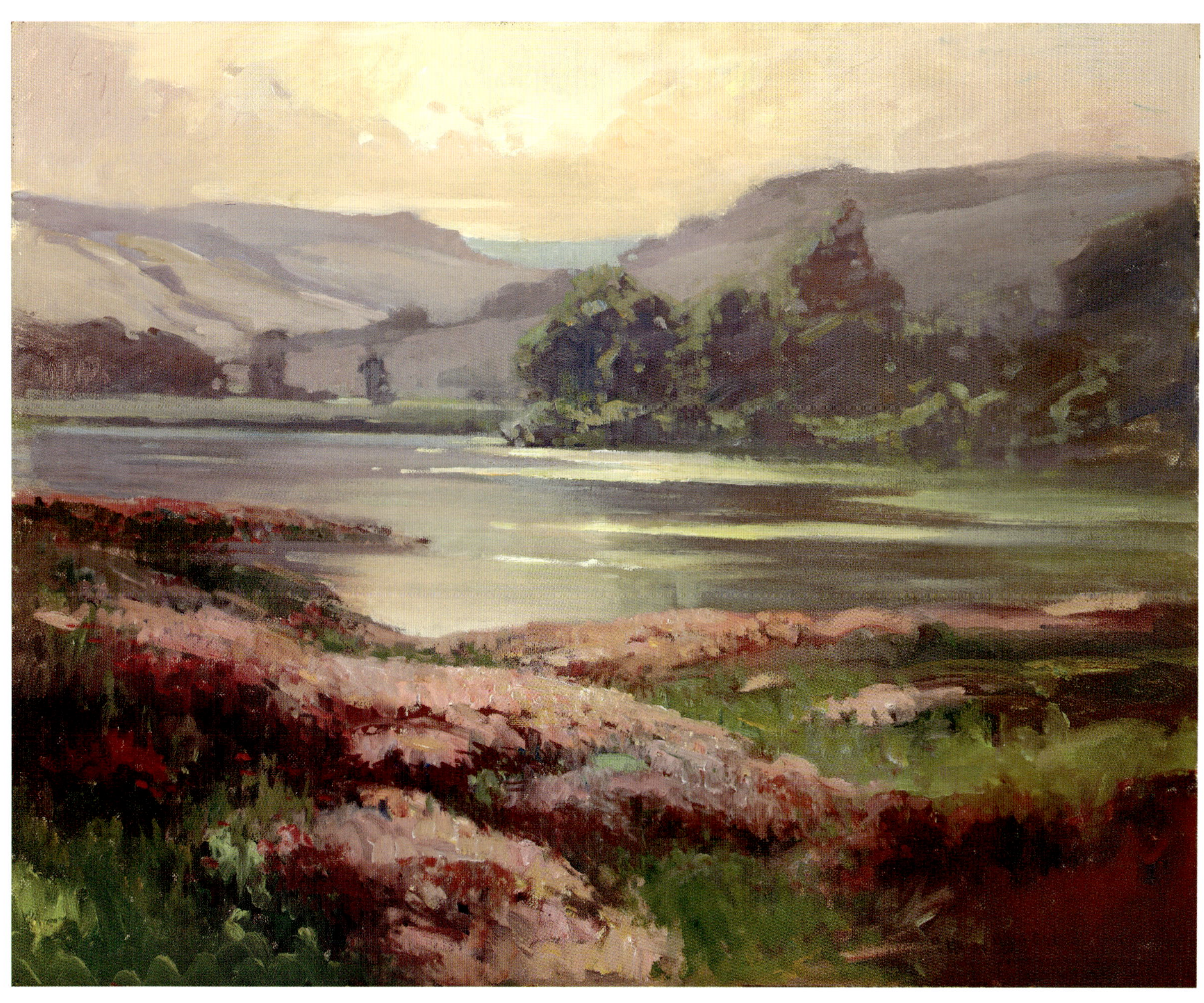

PLATE 35
Untitled (mountain lake), undated
Oil on Masonite, 30 × 36 inches
Collection of the Charles S. Hayes Family

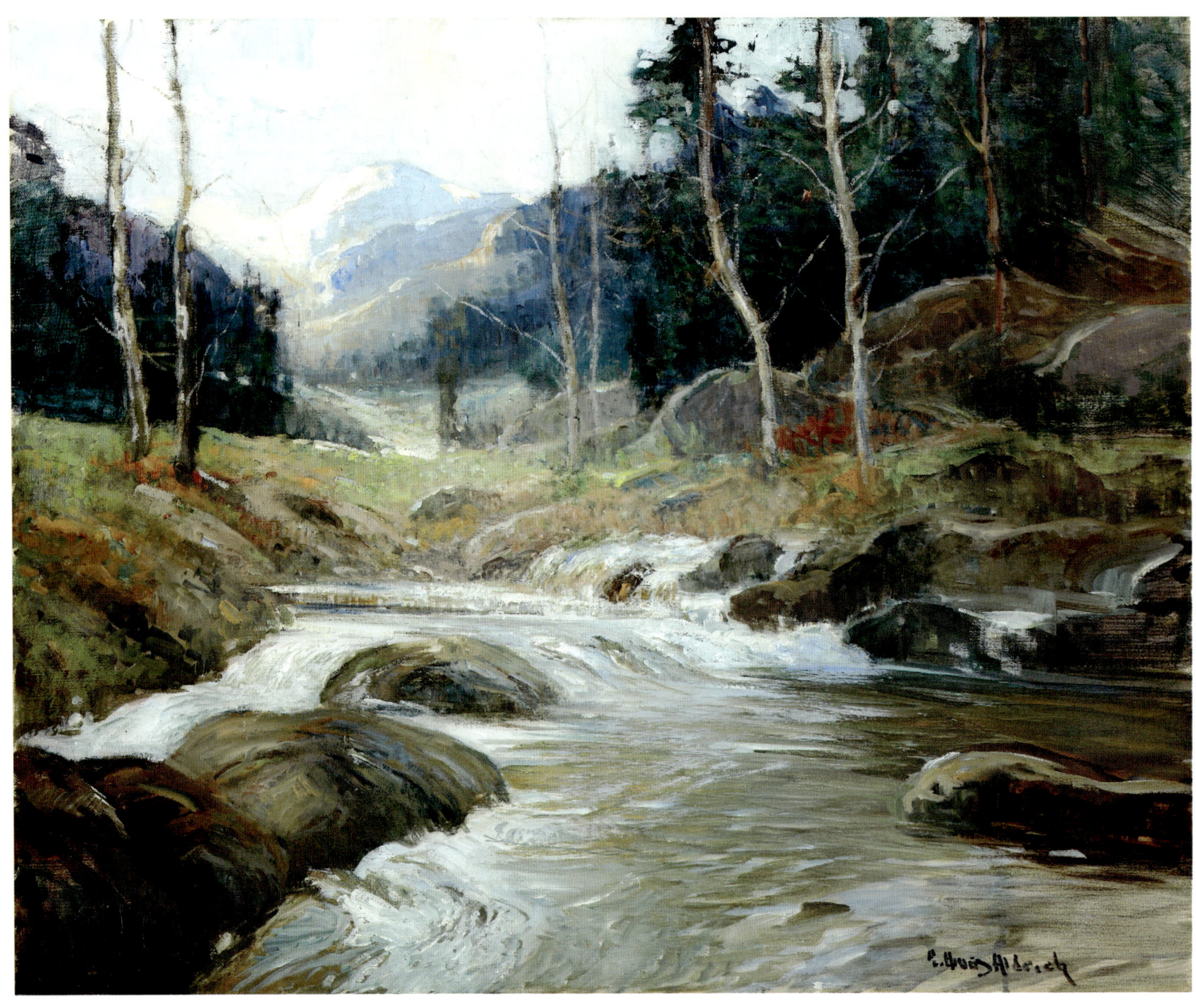

PLATE 36

Untitled (mountain river #1), undated

Oil on canvas, 25 × 30 inches

Private Collection

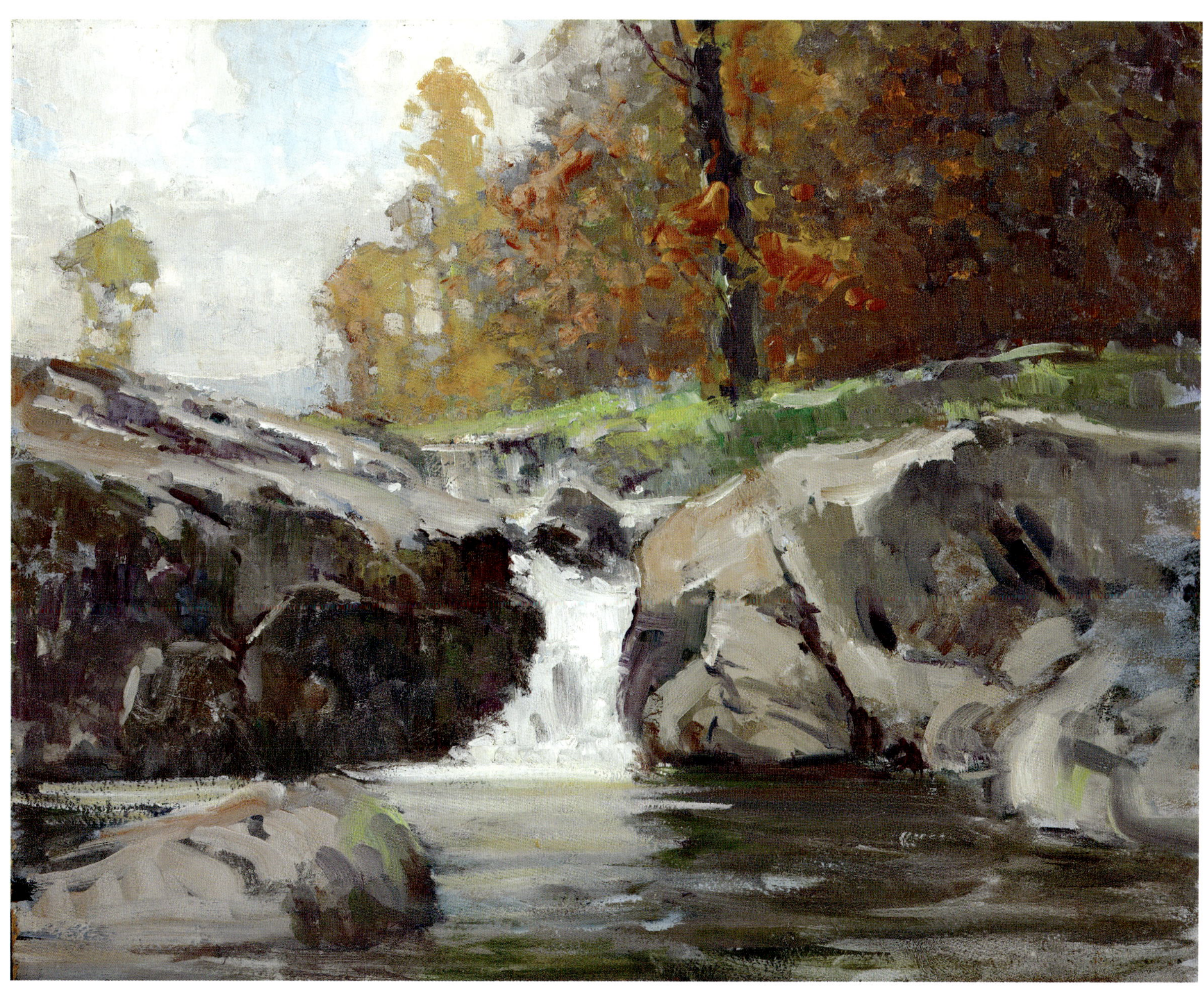

PLATE 37
Untitled (mountain river #2), undated
Oil on board, 14 ¾ × 18 ¼ inches
Collection of the Charles S. Hayes Family

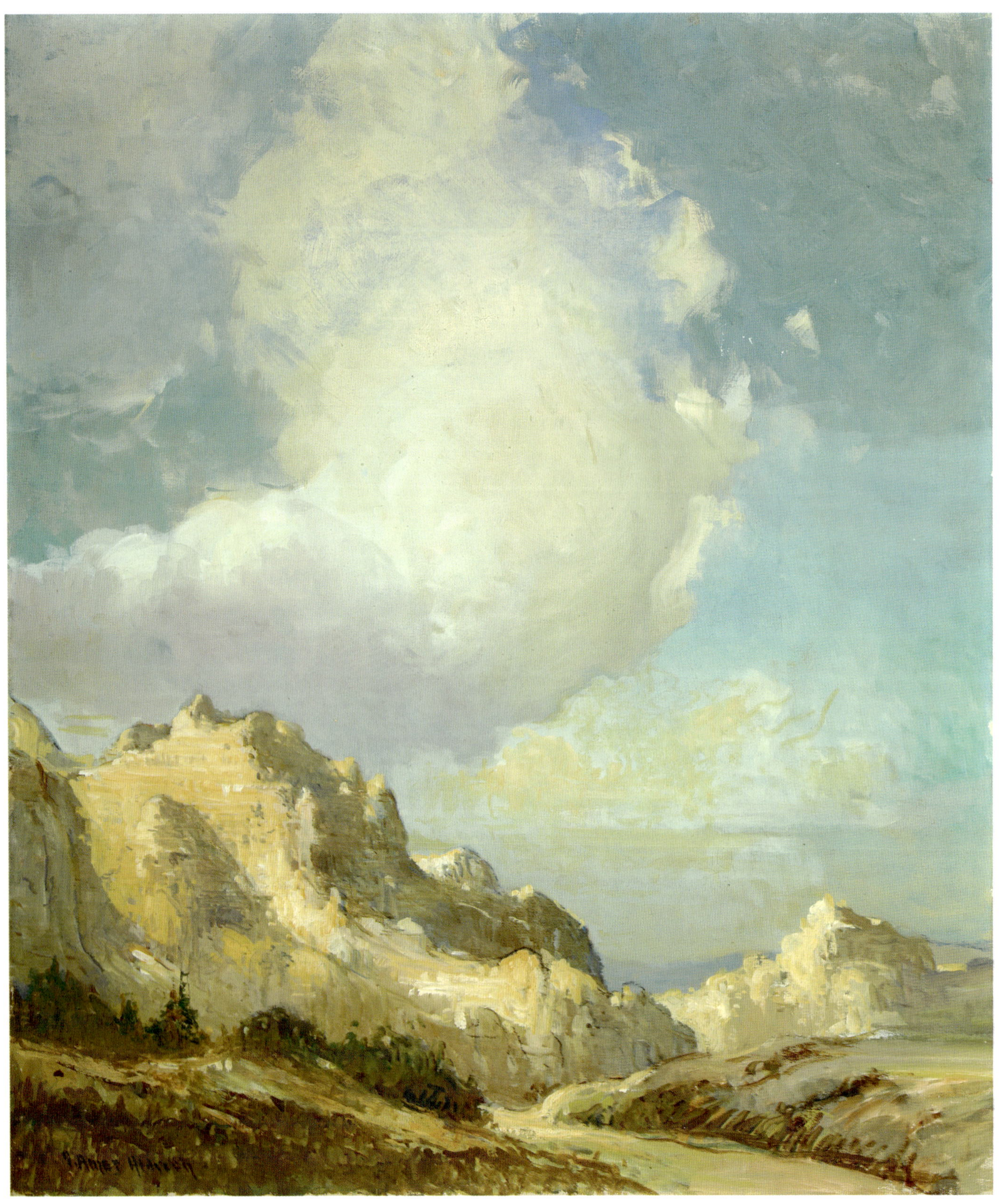

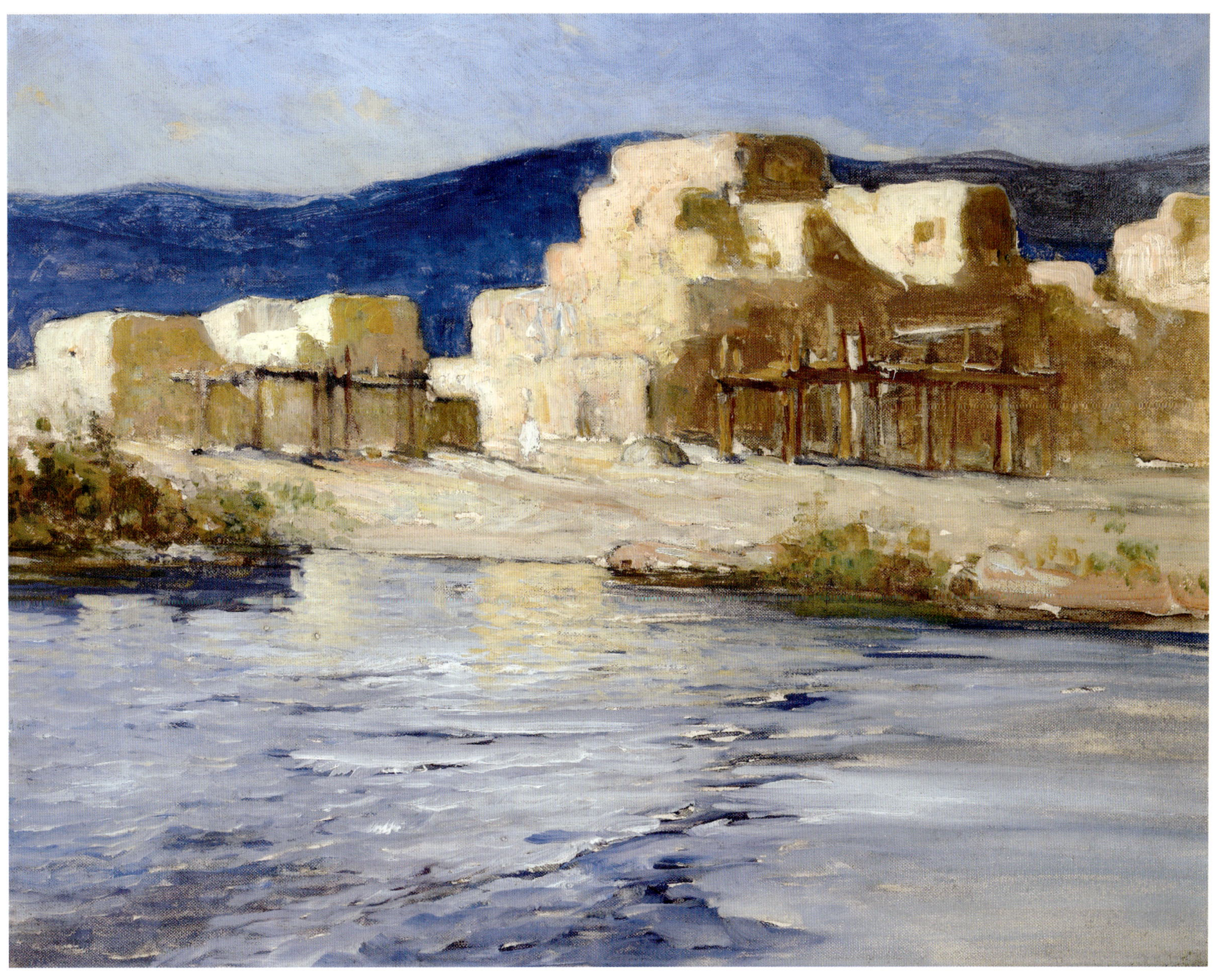

PLATE 38 {FACING}
Badlands, undated
Oil on canvas, 30 × 25 inches
Collection of the Saunders Family

PLATE 39
Untitled (Taos Pueblo), undated
Oil on canvas board, 16 × 20 inches
Collection of the Charles S. Hayes Family

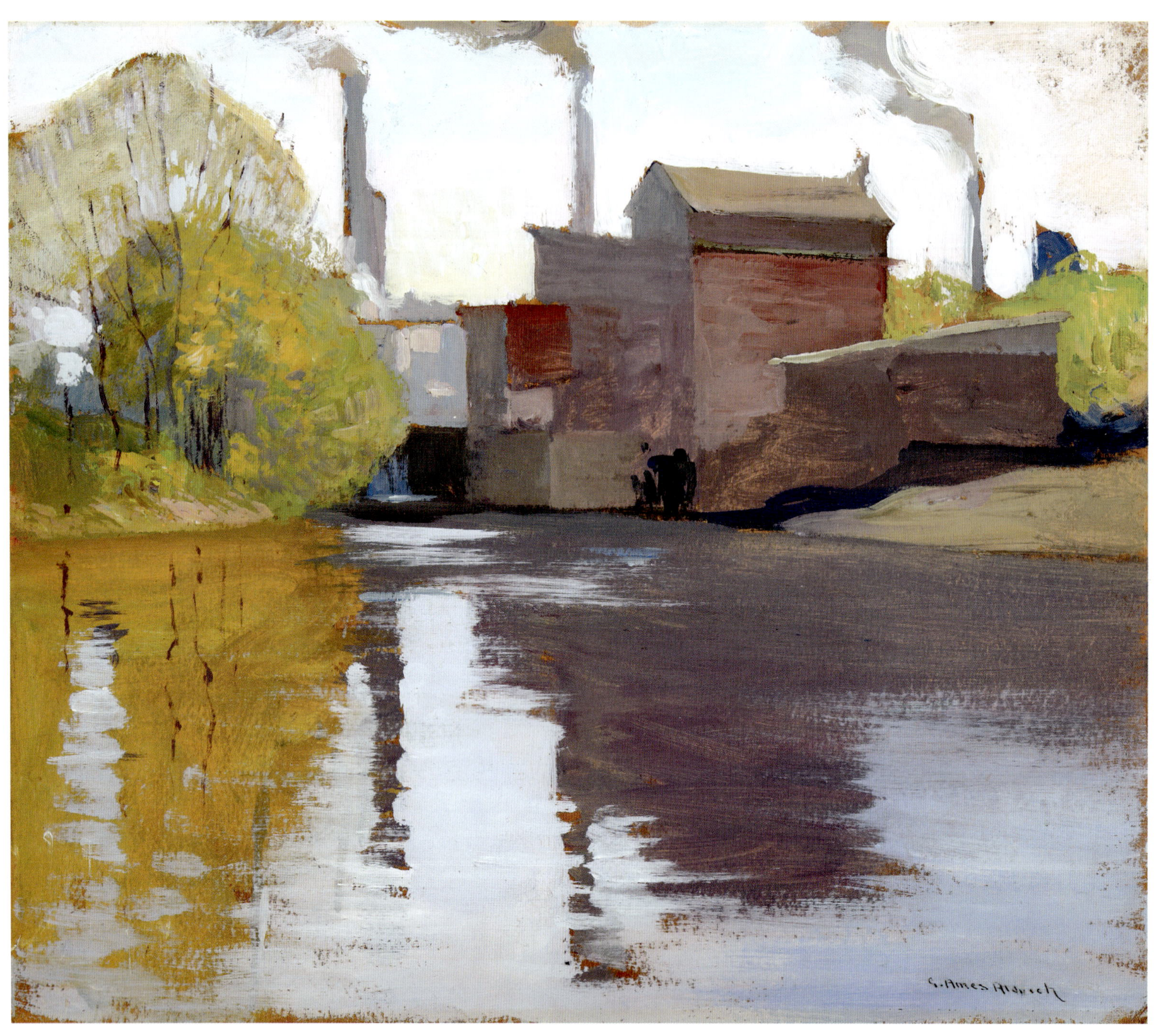

PLATE 40
Untitled (Ball-Band Plant #1), undated
Oil on canvas board, 12 × 16 inches
Collection of the Charles S. Hayes Family

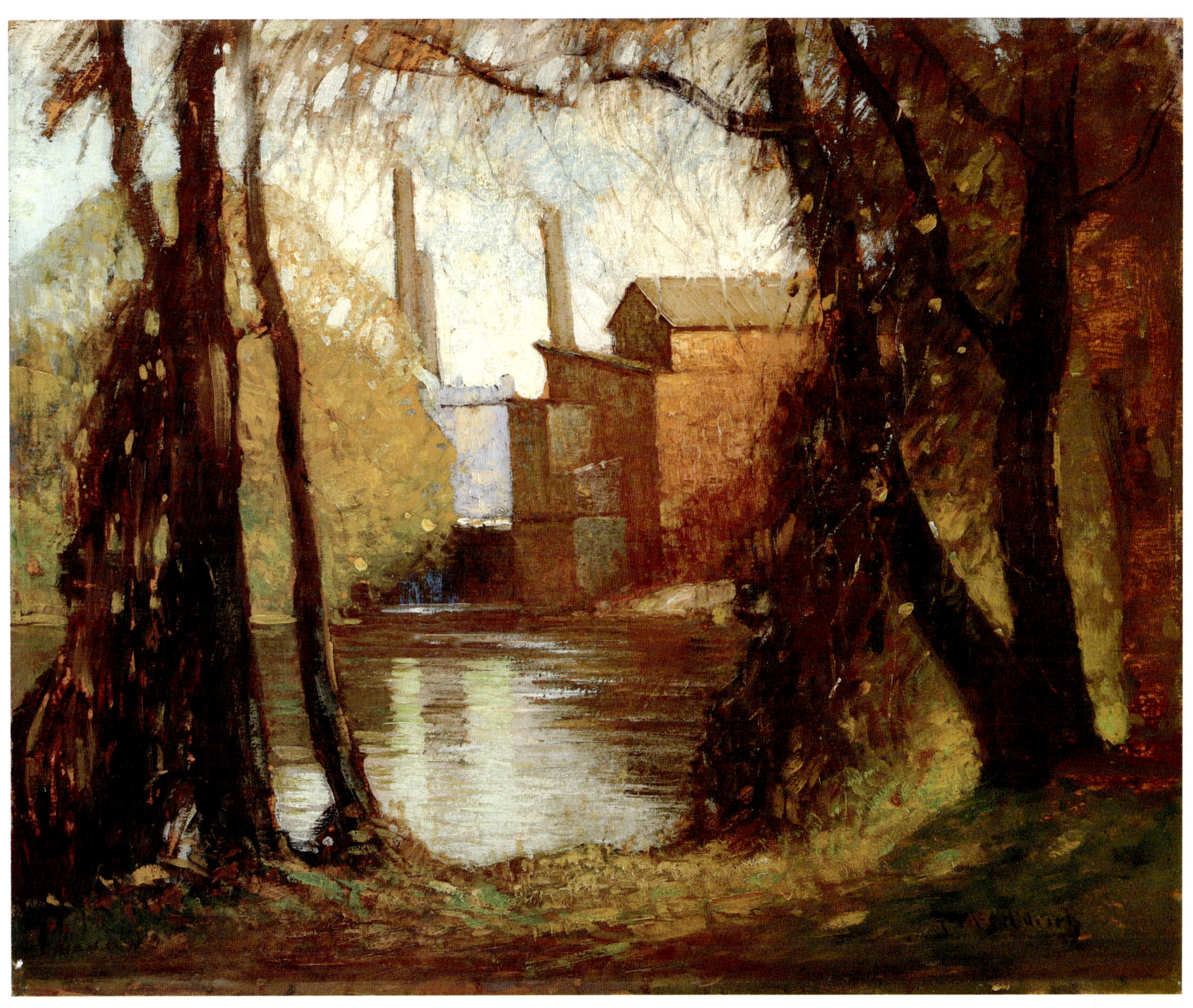

PLATE 41
Ball-Band Plant (#2), ca. 1920
Oil on board, 20 × 24 inches
Collection of Drs. Nicole and Todd Rozycki

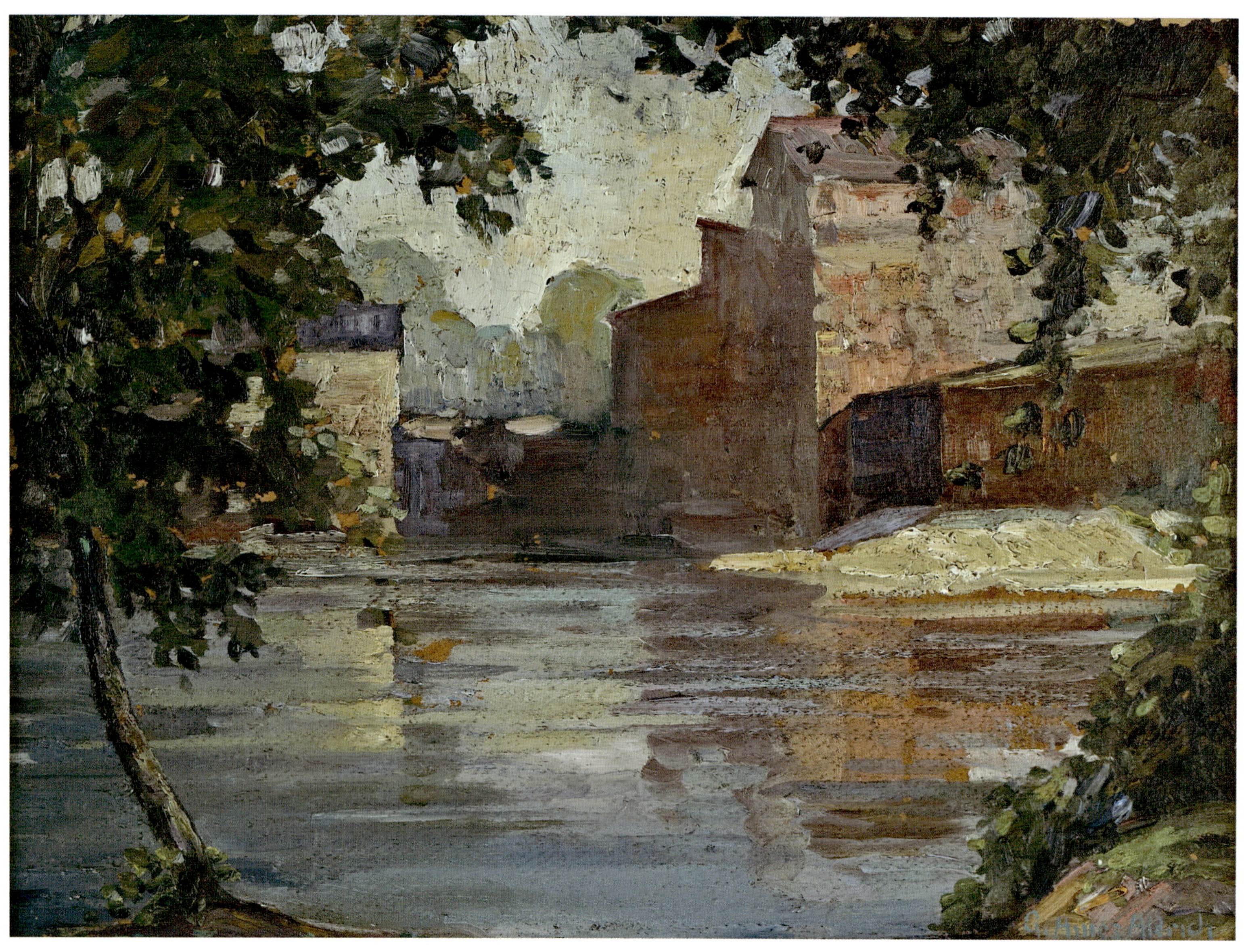

PLATE 42

Untitled (Ball-Band Plant #3), undated

Oil on board, 14 × 15 ¾ inches

Private Collection

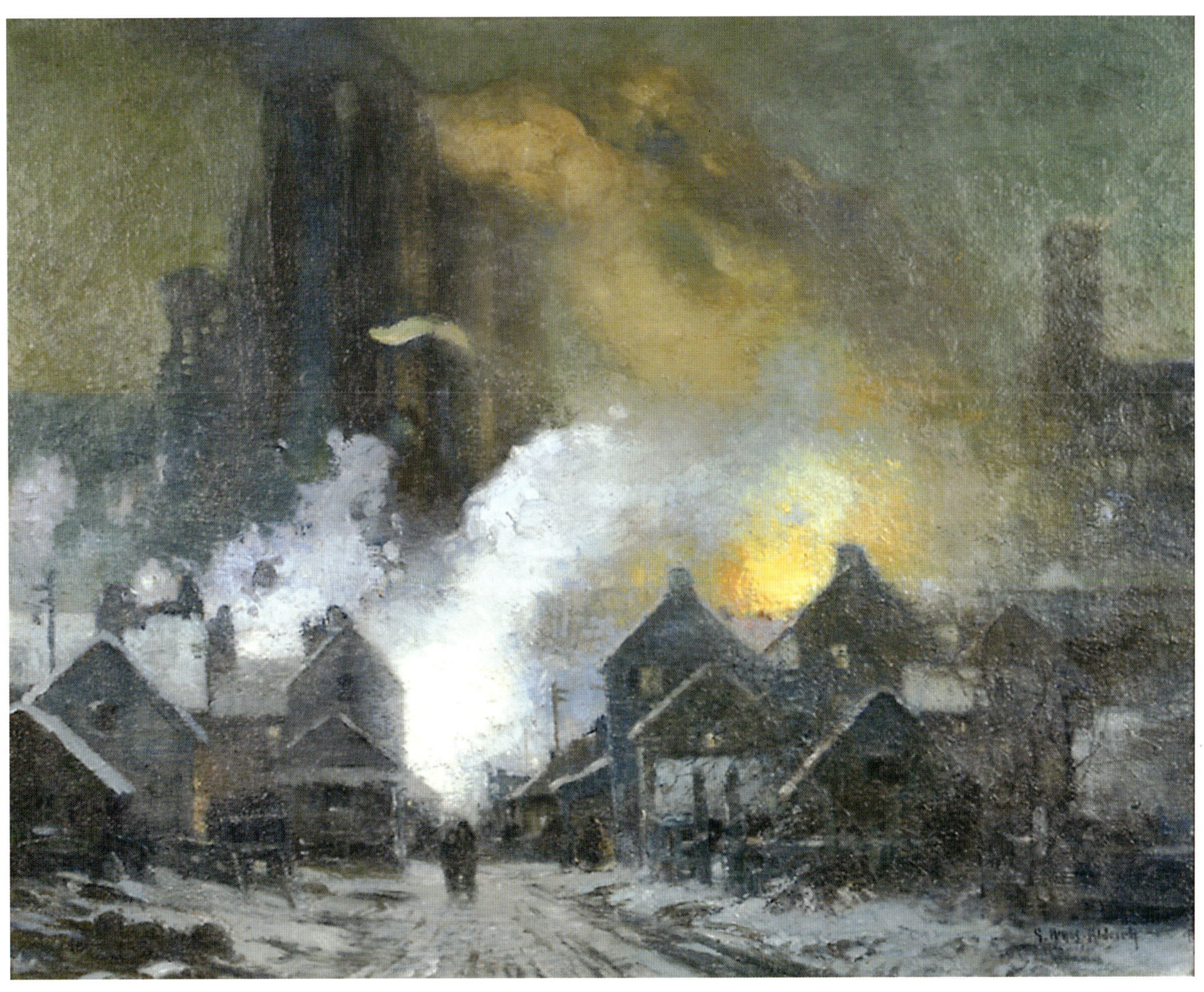

PLATE 43
The Melting Pot, Chicago, ca. 1926
Oil on canvas, 29 ¾ × 35 ¾ inches
Collection of Clifford Law Offices, Chicago

PLATE 44 {FOLLOWING}
Steel, undated
Oil on canvas, mounted on board, 39 × 39 inches
Collection of First Financial Bank, N. A.

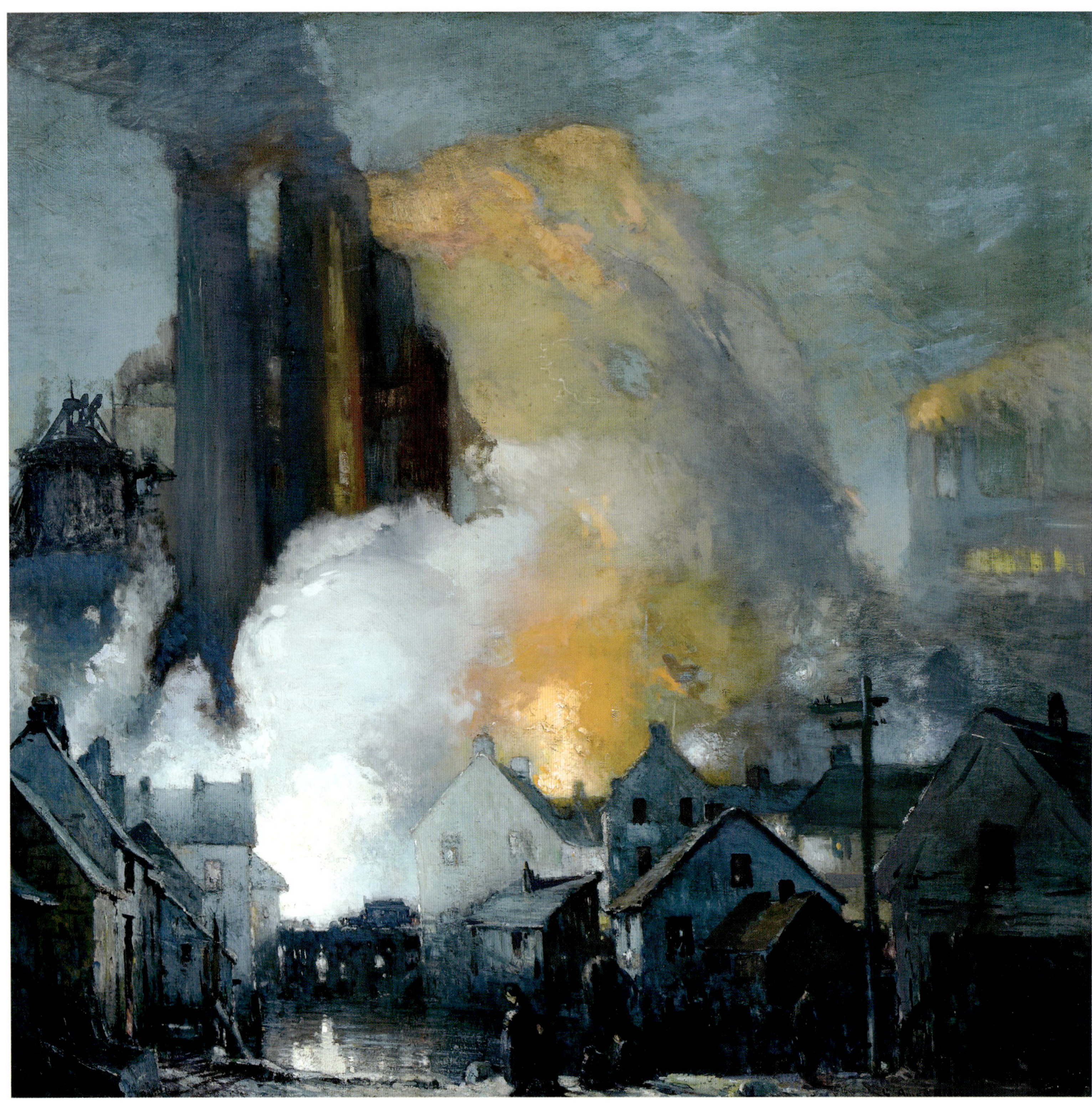

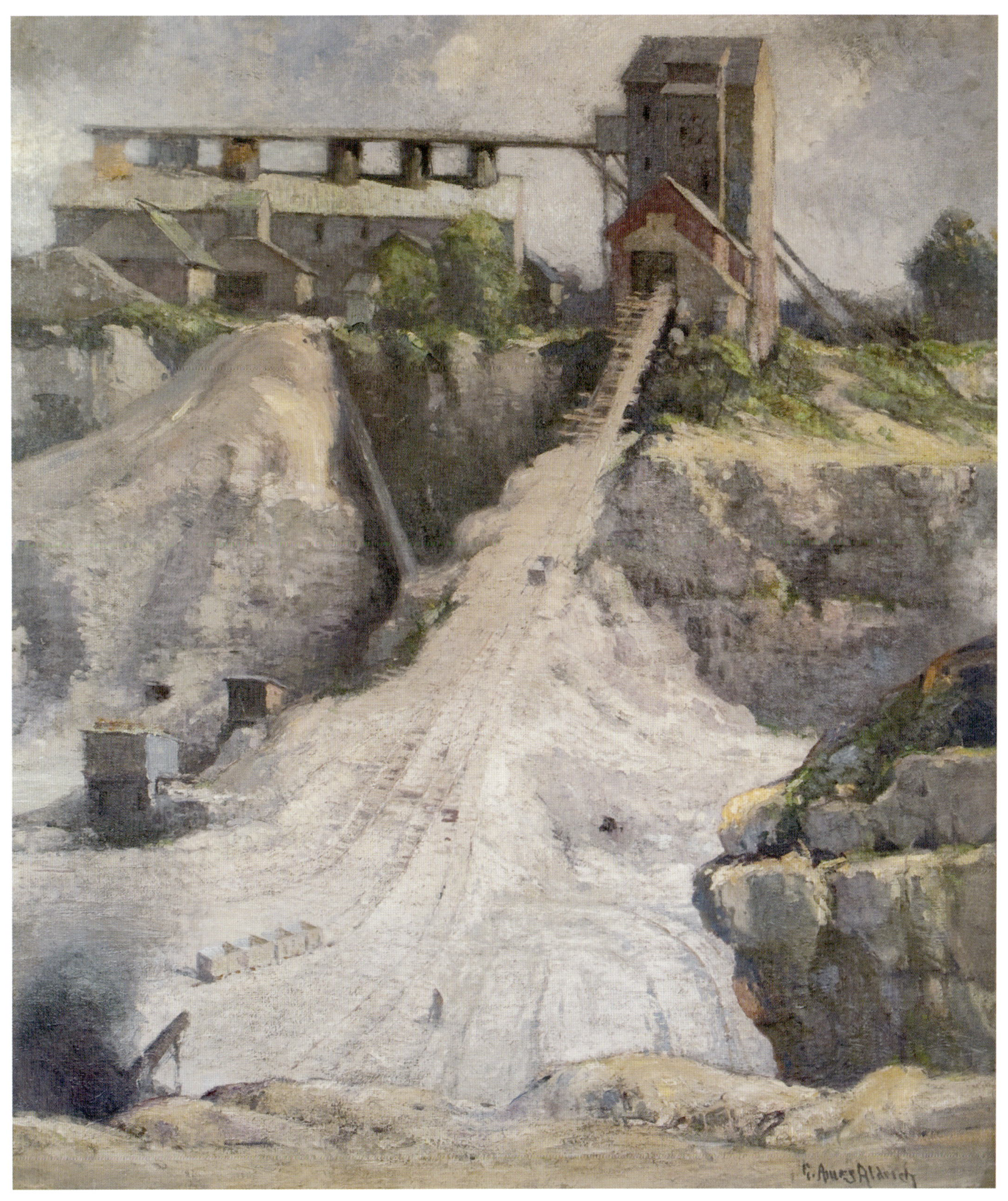
C. Ames Aldrich

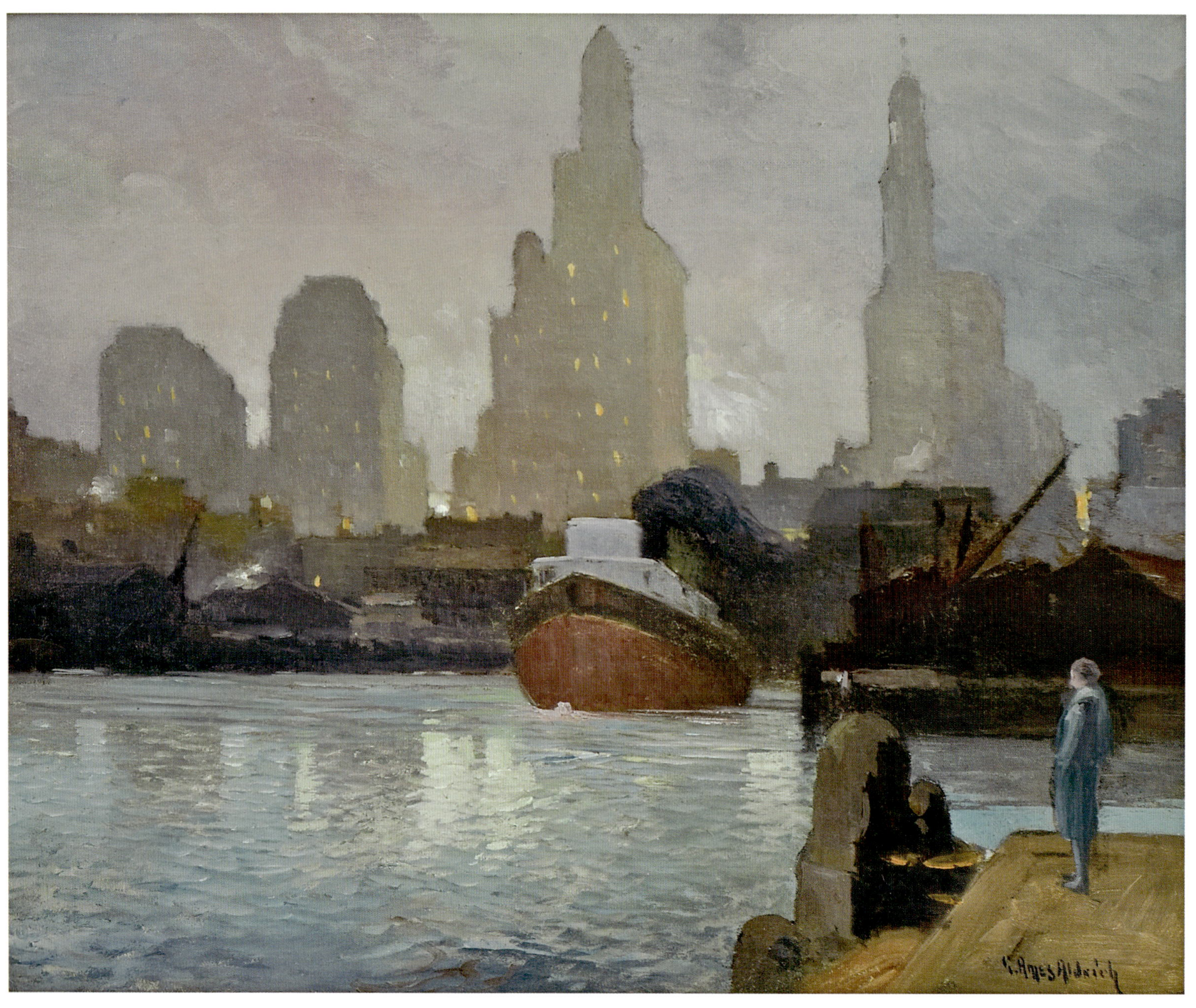

PLATE 45 {PRECEDING}
Quarries (Limestone Mine – Lyons, Illinois), ca. 1932
Oil on Masonite, 48 × 40 inches
Collection of Matthew M. Walsh

PLATE 46
Untitled (Chicago skyline), undated
Oil on board, 20 × 24 inches
Private Collection

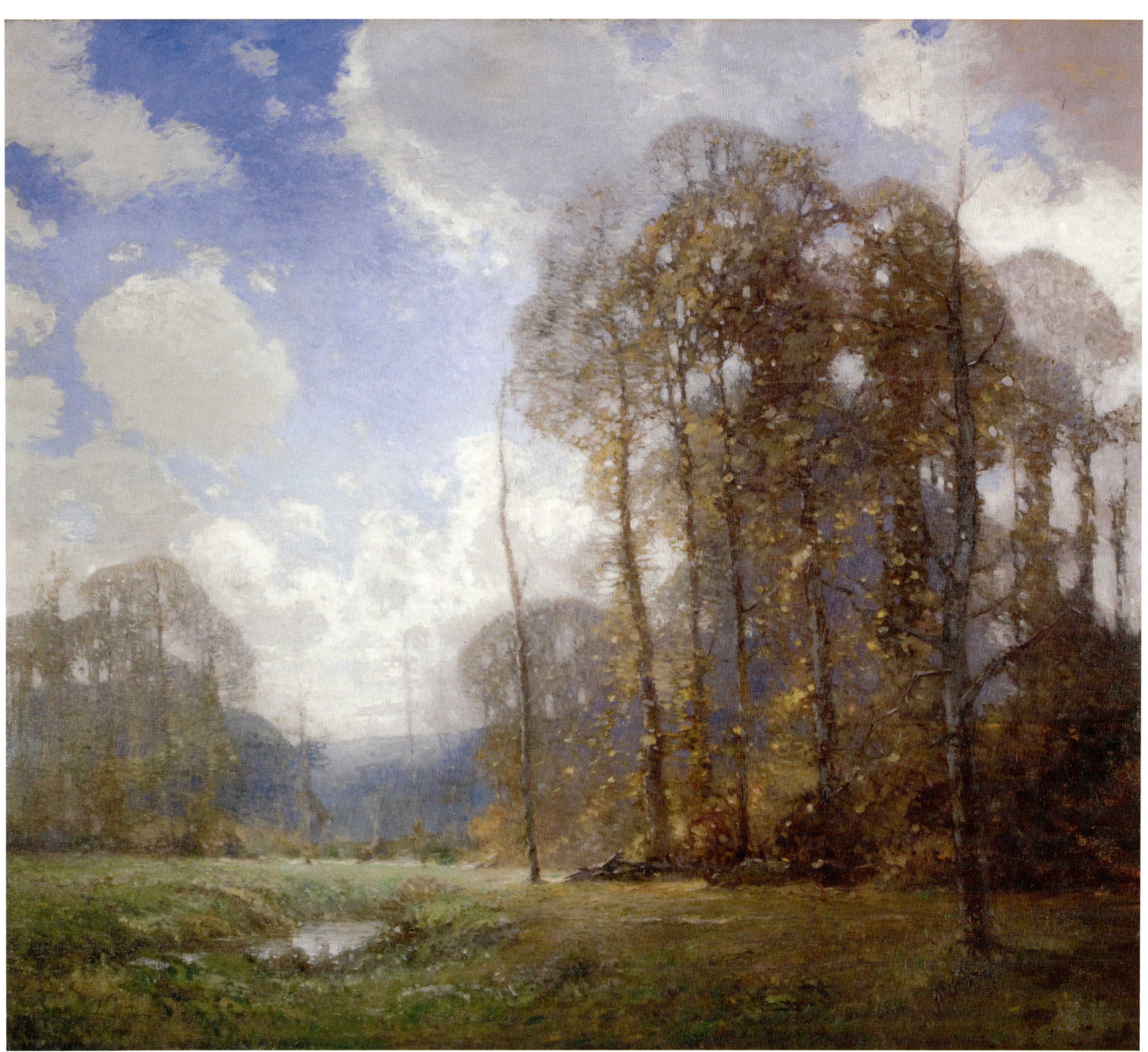

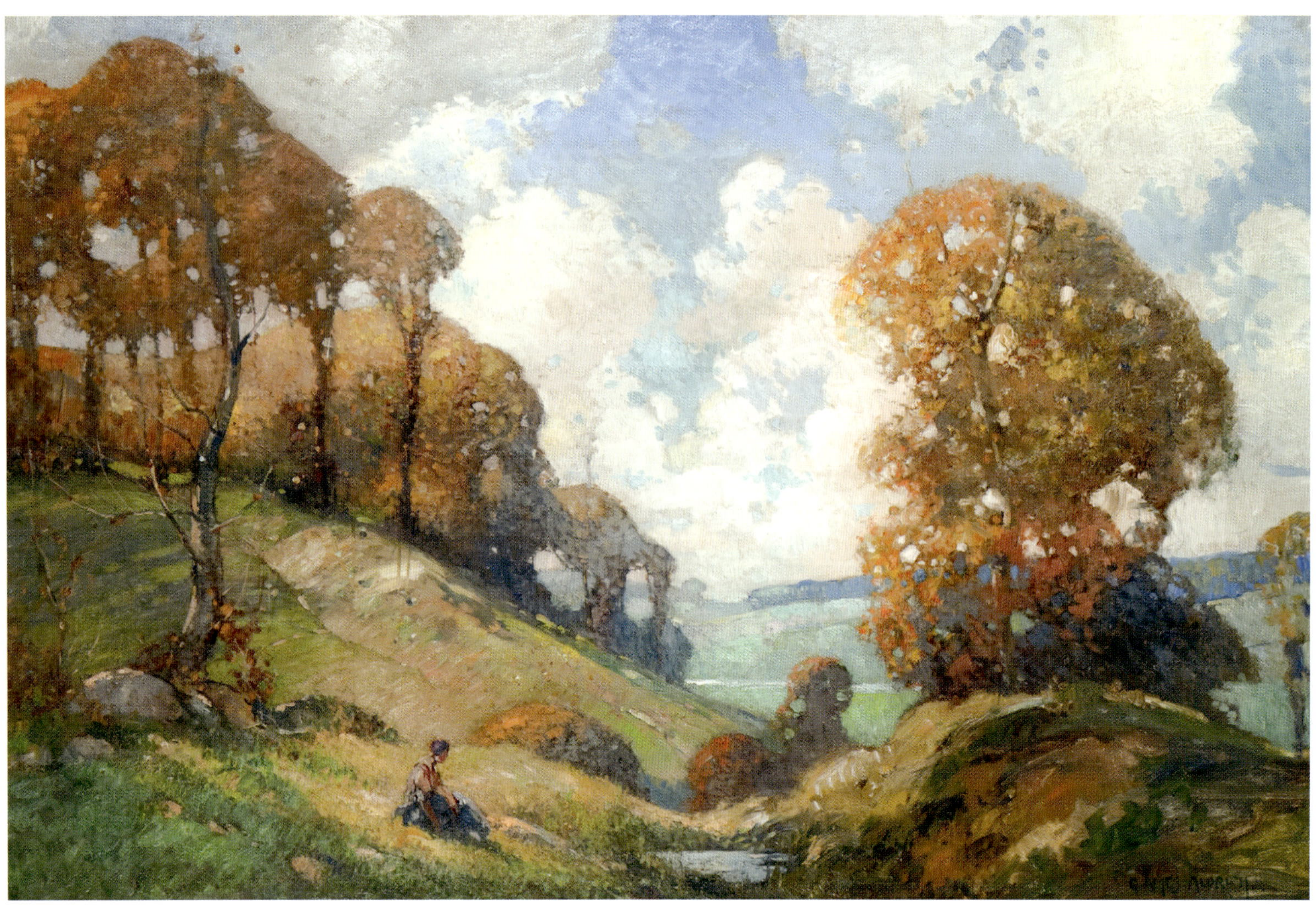

PLATE 47 {PRECEDING}
Untitled (pastoral scene), undated
Oil on board, 36 × 40 inches
Collection of Mary Toll and Bill Heimann

PLATE 48
Normandy Landscape, undated
Oil on canvas, 38 ¾ × 55 ¾ inches
Permanent Collection, Snite Museum of Art, University of Notre Dame, AA 1999.040

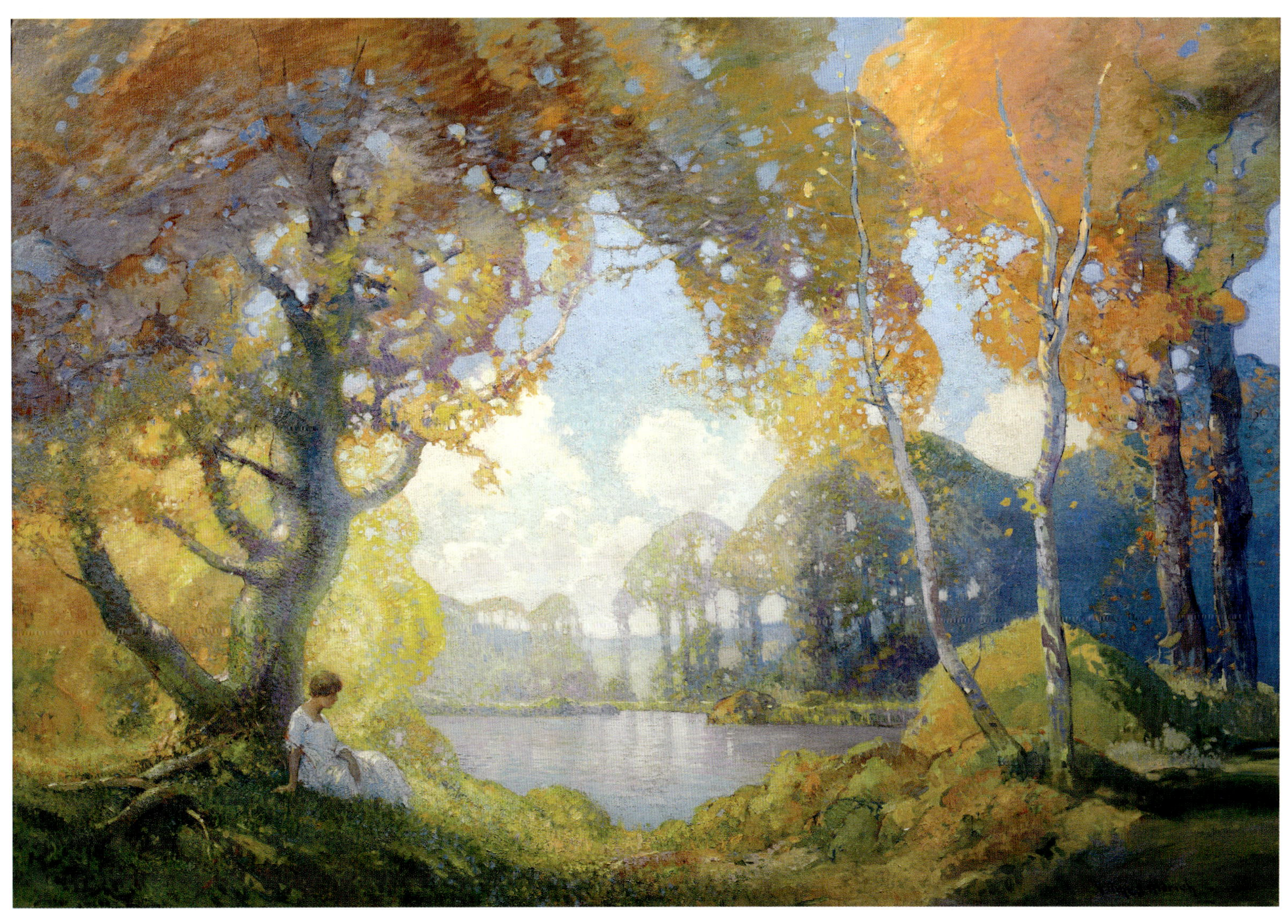

PLATE 49
Untitled (Oliver Hotel summer/fall landscape), undated
Oil on canvas, mounted on board, 67 × 92 inches
Collection of the Charles S. Hayes Family

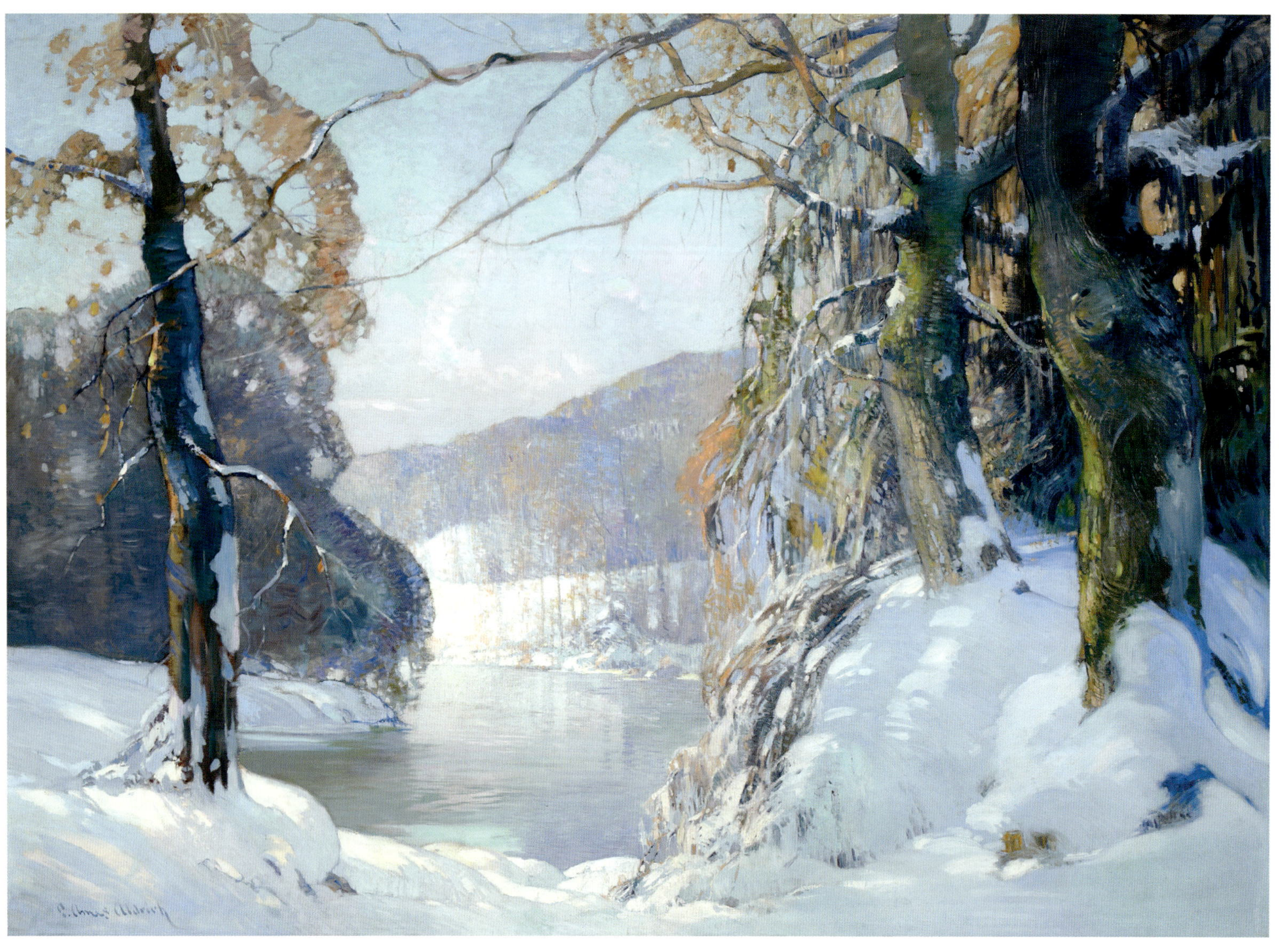

PLATE 50
Untitled (Oliver Hotel winter river scene), undated
Oil on canvas, mounted on board, 66 ½ × 90 ½ inches
South Bend Museum of Art, Gift of
National City Bank, 1999.4

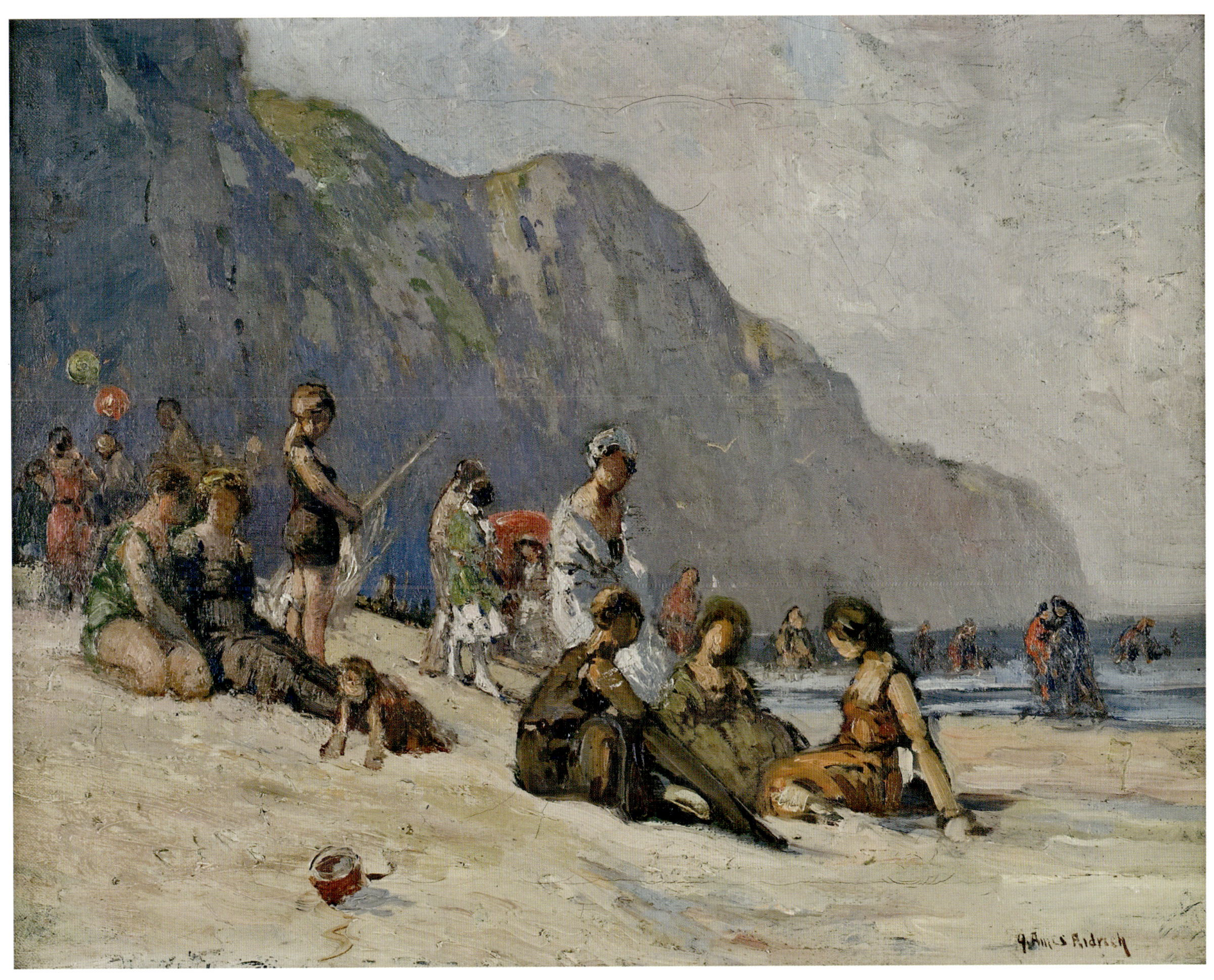

PLATE 51

Untitled (bathers on beach, France), undated

Oil on canvas, 16 ½ × 20 inches

Private Collection

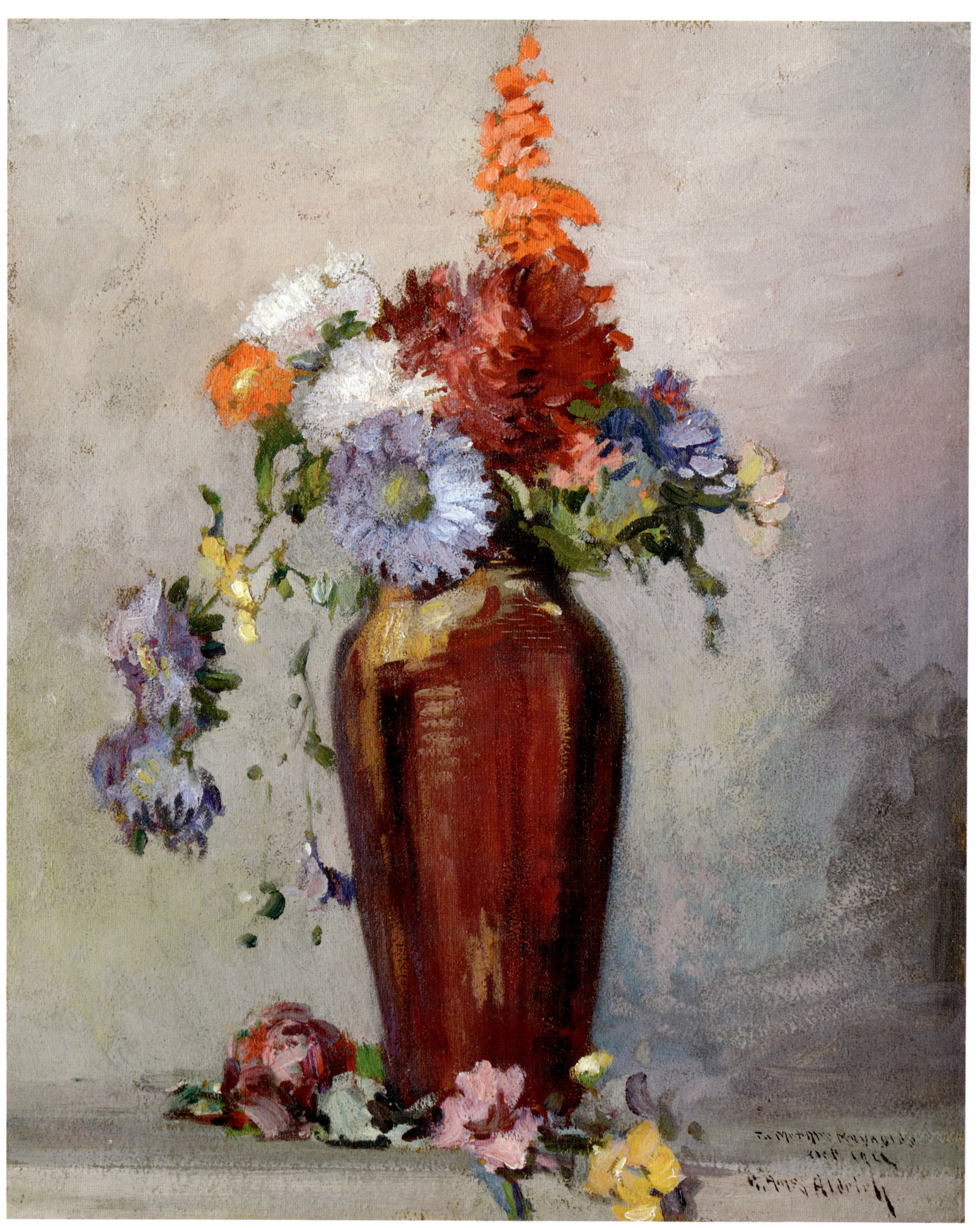

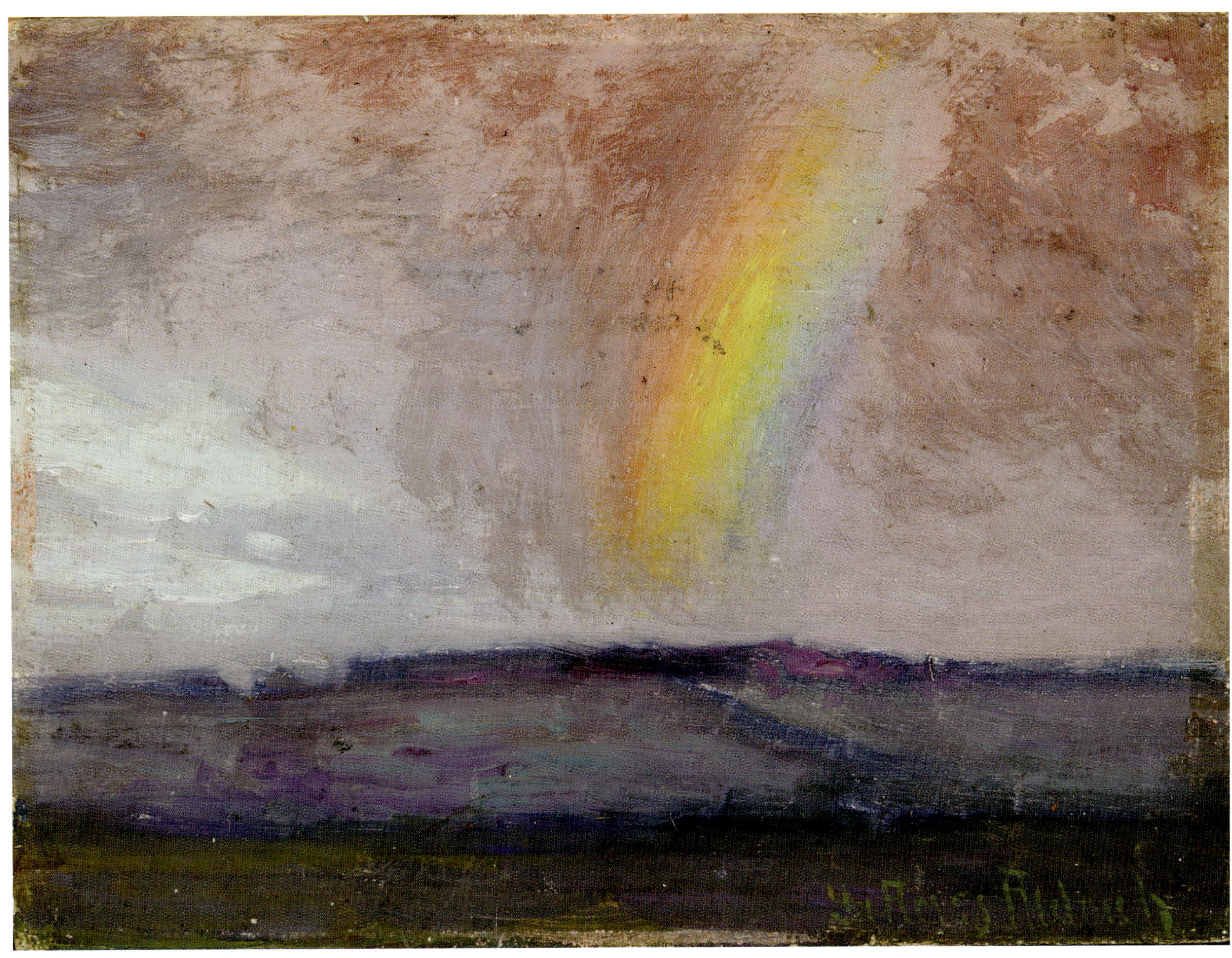

PLATE 52 {FACING}
Floral Still Life, ca. 1925
Oil on board, 20 × 16 inches
Collection of Drs. Nicole and Todd Rozycki

PLATE 53
Untitled (rainbow), undated
Oil on board, 5 × 7 inches
Bradley Vite Fine Arts

WENDY GREENHOUSE is an independent art historian who specializes in American art with a particular focus on the history of art in Chicago. She has co-authored catalogues for exhibitions on Archibald J. Motley, Jr., Frank Dudley, and Herman Menzel. Other publications include *Chicago Painting 1895 to 1945: The Powell and Barbara Bridges Collection,* the Terra Museum's *Chicago Modern, 1893–1945: Pursuit of the New,* and the catalogue of the Union League Club of Chicago art collection. Greenhouse earned her doctorate at Yale University.

GREGG HERTZLIEB is the director/curator of the Brauer Museum of Art at Valparaiso University in Valparaiso, Indiana. Hertzlieb has a master's degree in fine arts from the School of the Art Institute of Chicago and a master's degree in education from the University of Illinois at Chicago. Hertzlieb is the editor of *The Calumet Region: An American Place (Photographs by Gary Cialdella), Heeding the Voice of Heaven: Sadao Watanabe Biblical Stencil Prints,* and *Domestic Vision: Twenty-Five Years of the Art of Joel Sheesley,* as well as a contributor to *The Indiana Dunes Revealed: The Art of Frank V. Dudley.*

MICHAEL WRIGHT is an independent fine art consultant specializing in American art from 1900 to 1950.

This book was designed by Jamison Cockerham and set in type by Tony Brewer at Indiana University Press and printed at Four Colour Imports, Ltd.

The typefaces are Arno, designed by Robert Slimbach in 2007, and Penumbra Sans, designed by Lance Hidy in 1994, both issued by Adobe Systems, Inc.

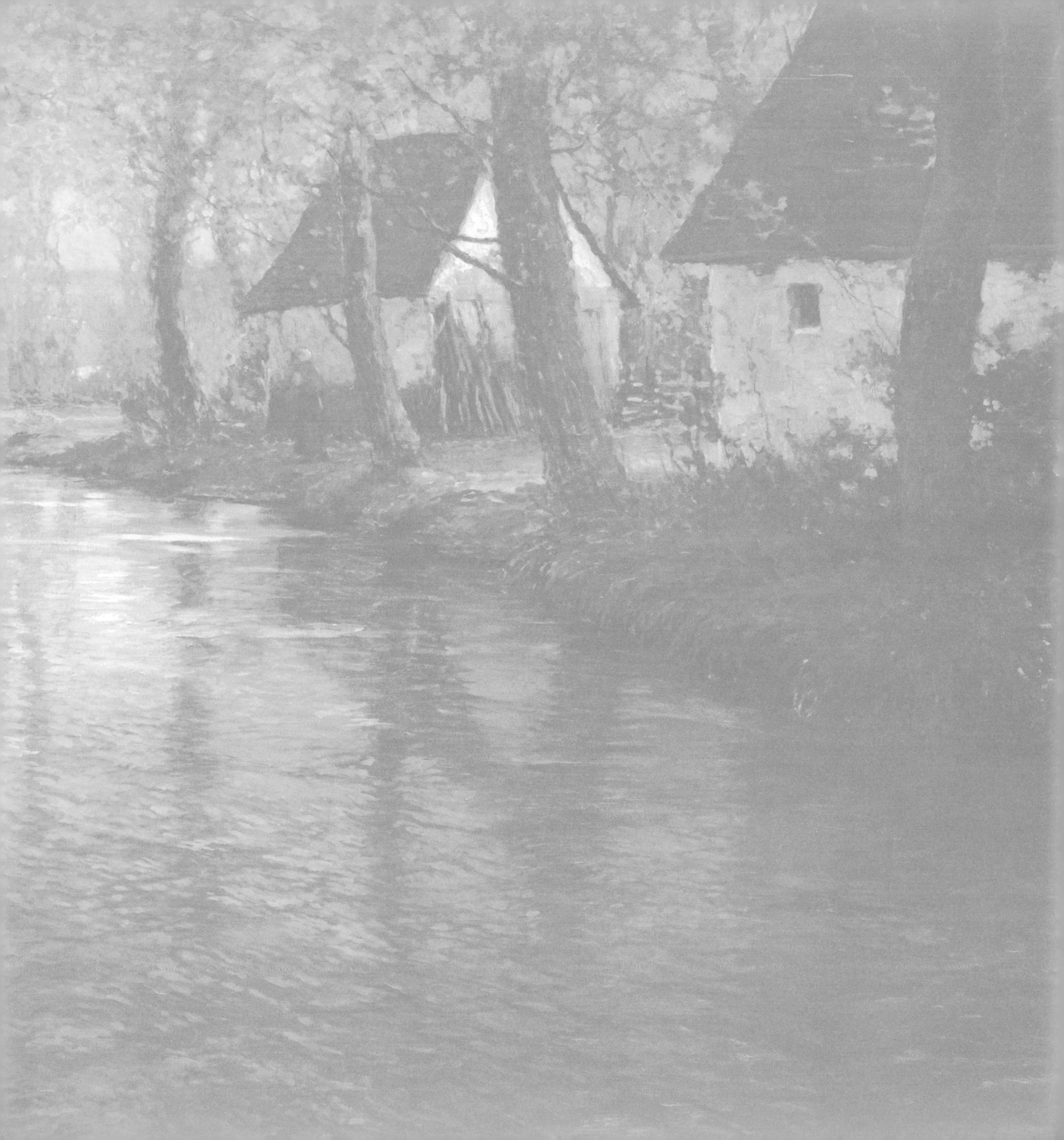

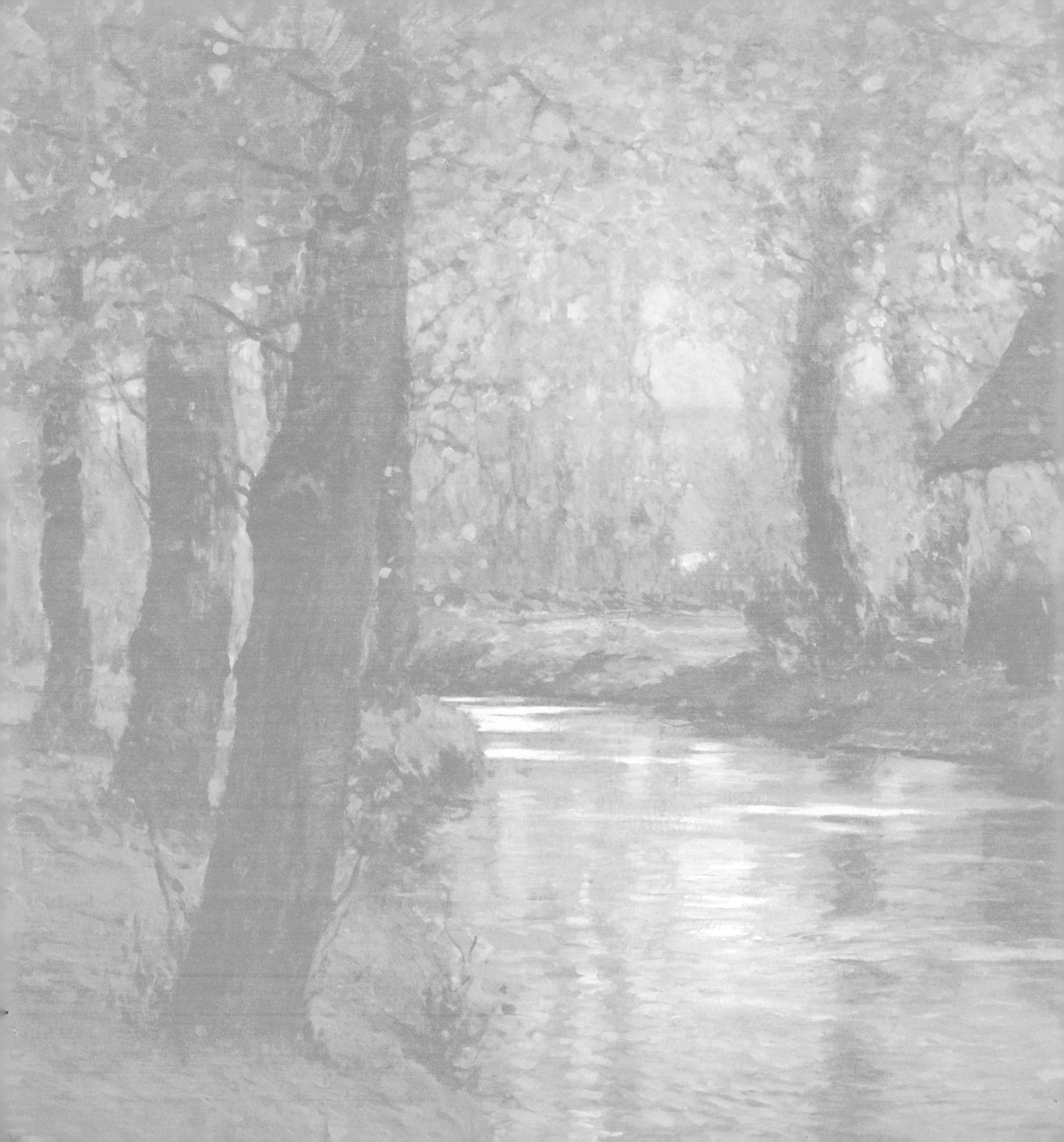